Fearless ON THE JOURNEY

Fulfilling the Purpose

Bishop Frances V. Mills
Rev. Arriana Mills Daniel

Fearless on the Journey

Fulfilling the Purpose

BISHOP FRANCES V. MILLS
REV. ARRIANA MILLS DANIEL

LITHONIA, GA

© 2019 – Frances V. Mills
All rights reserved.

No part of this publication may be reproduced, stored in a retrieval system or transmitted in any form or by any means, electronic, mechanical, photocopying, recording or otherwise, without the expressed written permission of the publisher.

Scripture references are taken from the King James Version of the Holy Bible unless otherwise noted.
Pronouns for referring to the Father, Son and Holy Spirit are capitalized intentionally and the words satan and devil are never capitalized.

Publisher:
MEWE, LLC
www.mewellc.com

First Edition
ISBN: 978-1-7324327-8-9

Library of Congress Control Number: 2019908021

Printed in the United States of America.

This book is dedicated first and foremost to my Lord and Savior who gave me the strength to push through my tears and my sorrow to put pen to paper to tell my baby's story.

To my husband, Ervin, who has suffered in silence the absence of his only daughter – "daddy's girl." To our only son, Ervin Allen Curtis Mills – Arriana's "big/little" brother who voluntarily donated his bone marrow to save his sister's life – which allowed her to go into remission and be with us for over a year.

And last but certainly not least, to my awesome Son-in-law, Mitch and my beautiful and strong grand babies, Christopher and Sydney, who have, through their strength and love, helped me to stand and move forward and live.

Thank you to my baby, my best friend, my daughter, Rev Arriana Mills Daniel, for your life, legacy and never-ending love that you gave, and we shared for your lifetime here on earth. To God be the glory!!

TABLE OF CONTENTS

Acknowledgements ix

Foreword xii

Introduction xiii

Part 1 – A Mother's Love on the Journey 1

    Ch. 1 – Fearless on the Journey 3

    Ch. 2 – The Battle Is Not Yours 11

    Ch. 3 – One More River to Cross 19

    Ch. 4 – Where Do We Go from Here? 37

    Ch. 5 – Last Part of the Journey 43

Part 2 – Sisters' Reflections of the Journey 47

    Ch. 6 – Reflection – Shayron Brown (cousin) 49

    Ch. 7 – Reflection – Stephanie V. Mills (cousin) 63

    Ch. 8 – Reflection – Carla Patrick (best friend) 67

Part 3 – Fearless on the Journey (A Daughter's Message to the World) 77

    Ch. 9 – Are You Anchored in the Lord? 79

    Ch. 10 – Holding Pattern 91

Part 4 – The Authors on the Journey 103

    About the Authors 105

Acknowledgements

I am grateful to the members of Tabernacle of Faith Christian Church for their support of the First Family during Rev. Arriana's illness and after her passing. Many, many thanks also to our immediate family and extended family, the many pastors and their members, our many friends, acquaintances and co-workers who have prayed for our family, who took care of us in so many ways and who still continue to lift us up in prayer. May God richly bless each of you is our humble prayer.

Foreword

For almost thirty years, God has blessed me with the honor to walk and serve closely with The Frances and Ervin Mills Family. Make no mistake about it, they are one in unity and purpose. Bishop Mills was one of the first females licensed and ordained to preach under my pastorate at The Greater Piney Grove Baptist Church, Atlanta. Her family and church was front and center with this ground breaking call to ministry. She also served as one of our first "paid" staff members.

Her mini-me, Arriana was always with her mother willing to learn and most of all to serve. She was a young lady that could fit into any role. In the church and out of the church. Her wedding to Mitch was a "Cinderella" moment.

One Sunday on Columbia Drive after I preached a challenging sermon, "Re" came forward and finally acknowledged her call to Christian ministry. There was not a dry eye in the church, **but** no one was surprised.

This book, this testimonial will serve as a memorial to Arriana. But also, it will encourage hundreds and thousands who must face challenges in their lives despite being called and as Arriana's name meant "holy." This is a must read and needs to be promoted by all in the faith community because God wants us to fulfill our purpose on this journey of faith.

Rev. Dr. William E. Flippin, Sr., Senior Pastor
The Greater Piney Grove Baptist Church, Atlanta
Founder, The Flippin Legacy Ministries

INTRODUCTION

This writing is an attempt to capture the life story of my daughter, Rev. Arriana Letrecia Mills Daniel. Her battle with Leukemia was short, but it was a powerful testimony of her commitment to serving the Lord no matter the circumstance. Rev. Arriana was my first-born child, my only daughter, my friend, my confidante, my twin in the spirit and one whom I loved with all my heart and soul. Most people described her as my "mini me." She was the one person I depended on for encouragement and sound advice when I served as senior pastor of Tabernacle of Faith Christian Church. She served in her role as assistant pastor in service to God's people.

Arriana was wise beyond her years. But more than that, God had gifted her with "wisdom and knowledge" about so many things. She was an amazing person. No one could figure out how she knew so much about everything, and she would always say, "I don't know where it comes from – God just gives it to me."

Arriana was beautiful in every way – mind, body, and spirit. She had gorgeous looks, a shapely body, long legs, wide hips, tiny waist, beautiful smile, and bouncy, flowing hair that was always shiny and cut in an attractive style.

Arriana was stylish; she loved fashionable clothes, shoes, and jewelry to match. When she walked into a room, heads would definitely turn. She was fairly tall (about 5' 4"); she walked with her head held high and her shoulders back as her hips swayed from side to side. Her body moved with the elegance of a runway model. Yes, when she entered a room, she caught your eye and commanded your attention. And if you didn't know her, soon you would be asking, "Who is that young lady?" But along with her outer beauty came a beautiful spirit-filled, anointed, woman of God who was saved, sanctified, and filled with the Holy Ghost. Rev. Arriana was truly a child of the King, sold out to Jesus and would let it be known everywhere she went.

While Rev. Arriana made her presence known in the Christian community as a preacher, teacher, singer, praise and worship leader, as well as a servant of almighty God, she was also well known and respected in the business community. She held a bachelor's degree in Business Administration from the University of Georgia and a master's degree in Human Resources Management from Keller Graduate School. Additionally, she was president and CEO of two businesses she founded: "Fashions by Nichelle" and "Emerging Visions Training & Consulting, Inc." All of this was done while she managed her household as the wife to Mitch Daniel for 16 years and mother of Sydney (10) and Christopher (13) at the time of her passing. From 1985 until 2015, Rev. Arriana had a professional career in higher education. Her last position being dean and division director at Atlanta Technical College where she managed eight divisions and approximately ninety employees. Wow, what a life!

This book is an attempt to encourage your faith in God – no matter what the circumstances. It is an effort to share the testimony of a "sweet and powerful voice," which has been silenced but yet speaks. It's also an attempt to give the reader a glimpse of the life, legacy, and journey of a young wife, mother, servant of God, business woman, career professional, preacher, teacher, singer, writer, and faith-filled woman of God who was obedient to God and served Him with her whole heart, mind, body, and soul. She was truly sold out to Him. She loved the Lord and kept her faith in Him through the many storms of life she encountered, even in the final storm when she knew she would come through but not on this side of glory. Through it all and knowing how her story would "begin," she never gave up hope but trusted God all the way from earth to glory. Her faith was rooted in Him until the sweet, sweet end of life as we know it on this side of heaven ended. But as she told me so many times, "This is just part of my journey." Her journey has not ended; it has only just begun. I pray you'll be encouraged and blessed as you go through the journey with her.

Bishop Frances V. Mills

PART 1

A Mother's Love on the Journey

CHAPTER 1

FEARLESS ON THE JOURNEY

Rev. Arriana Letrecia Mills Daniel's life journey began on Saturday, February 3, 1967, when she was born. Her life here on earth ended on Monday, October 23, 2017, but she has transcended to eternal life in heaven forever. It's only just begun.

Arriana was born to a young 19-year-old couple who knew absolutely nothing about taking care of a baby, but they were absolutely crazy in love with each other. They knew they had been blessed with an angel, a little girl whom they named "Arriana," which means very holy.

Before she was delivered, the doctors gave her daddy some grim news. He said there were complications, and it looked as if they might not have been able to save both Mom and baby. He had to decide which one would live in the event they had to choose. Her dad's answer was – both!

God heard his cry, and we both came through the ordeal, but I remained very sick for weeks. Thus, we both remained in the hospital for an extended time until we could come home together. The devil tried to kill Arriana before she could make her entrance into the world, but God had a plan. She was holy.

As Arriana grew up, everybody knew she was a special little girl. She was always much more mature in her actions and words than children her age. She was responsible and ambitious, always trying to do the right thing – well, at least, most of the time. There were times when she was a typical mischievous, little girl who had to get the proverbial spanking – but not often. When she did do wrong, a remorseful look would come over her. Tears would flow and the fear in her little eyes made it difficult to spank her and cause her more pain, so we had to find other methods of punishment. I guess it was all because we knew or sensed she was holy.

Her father and I wanted only the best for our little girl. We tried to give her the best of everything that was within our power – the best clothes, the best training (piano lessons, every type of sports activity she wanted to try, singing, acting – whatever she desired).

When it was time for her to go to school, we enrolled her in a private Catholic school even though we knew nothing about Catholicism. We only knew that this particular school was one of the best in Dekalb County. And Arriana excelled! She was loved by all the nuns. She had lots of friends at her school and was showing signs she would be a real leader; she was fearless. However, after a few years, the school implemented a new rule, because the wait list was growing longer each year. They decided to give Catholics, especially members of their diocese first preference for enrollment, so we

(Baptist) had to find another school for our children. We had to enroll Arriana in public school.

Public school was a piece of cake for our baby. She was far ahead of her classmates in every subject. She tested on the next grade level, and the school wanted her to skip a level. Her dad and I were extremely proud of her, and it was a hard decision to make. We decided to let her remain with her class and be an "A" student, rather than skip her to the next level and possibly struggle in some areas down the road. Once again, she proved just how fearless she was. She was not afraid to tackle anything and was chosen to participate in everything at the school. She would take lead roles in plays, assist the teachers, be in the school patrol, chorus, and, of course – on the honor roll.

By the time Arriana turned 5, her dad and I were expecting our second bundle of joy – Ervin Allen Curtis Mills. When Ervin was born, Arriana was ecstatic. She had a baby brother, a playmate. She watched over him, helped take care of him and protected him from anybody who got too close to her baby brother. By the time he entered elementary school, she was like a little mother hen. She walked him to his classes before going to hers. She waited for him, so they could be together coming home. One day, as they were walking home, a 5th-grade boy was picking on Ervin and made him cry. Arriana used her expensive umbrella (it was a Totes – fairly expensive in those days) to beat the boy down and ran him home. Over the years, that young man has brought us to tears many times as we laughed at the way he described how Arriana beat him up with an umbrella. When we asked her why she started a fight with the young man, she would simply reply, "He shouldn't have bothered Ervin because Ervin wasn't bothering him. Besides, he was bigger than Ervin. He should have picked on somebody his age." It didn't occur to her that she might get in trouble for fighting or tearing up that expensive almost new umbrella.

High school was more of the same for Arriana. Oh, she didn't get into any more fights, but she tackled new experiences and excelled in everything she attempted. She tried out for Junior Varsity Cheerleaders and made it, not only as a squad member but the captain. In her second year of being on the JV Cheerleader team, she was chosen to also cheer with the Varsity team. By the 10th-grade year, she was on the Varsity Cheerleader team and was co-captain. She was the first 10th-grader to make co-captain (usually a junior or senior held this title). By her junior year, she was captain and remained in that position throughout her senior year as well.

Arriana also tried out for the drama club and received the lead role in the school's first major production to become a School of the Arts. The play was called the "Wizard of Oz," and she was chosen to play Dorothy – a singing, dancing, and acting role. She received standing ovations every night of the production. Needless to say, the school was deemed a School of the Arts and remains such to this day. From her 10th-grade year until graduation, Arriana participated in the school chorus, was a majorette in the band and was captain of majorettes. Amazingly, while participating in all these school activities, Arriana maintained her honor roll status. She was also active in her church, The Greater Piney Grove Baptist Church, serving in leadership roles in the junior choir and junior ushers. She participated in talent shows and beauty pageants both at church and school; she won those as well. Yes, Ms. Arriana Mills was a force to be reckoned with. She was determined to be the best, be a winner, be active, and achieve her goals.

Arriana graduated with many honors and many college acceptance letters – she chose UGA. As she matriculated through college, her goal was to own her business; thus, her major was business administration. Once she completed her undergraduate studies and received her bachelor's degree in Business, she set her sights on getting her Masters. This she did while working a full-time job. In the business world, she held several director positions at various technical schools.

As mentioned earlier, in her last position, she was the dean over eight departments at Atlanta Technical College managing approximately ninety employees. During the years of her professional advancement, Arriana got married, had two children, and started two businesses – her lifelong ambition. Additionally, she accepted God's call on her life to become a minister of the gospel. She was a licensed and ordained minister of the gospel and held several leadership positions in her church, Tabernacle of Faith Christian Church. She served as the assistant pastor, minister of music, director of children's church and a member of the governing board of the church.

Rev. Arriana managed every one of her roles in life with a spirit of commitment, dedication, fervency, grace, wisdom, and a wealth of knowledge but most of all, with love. Everybody who knew her would ask her how she got it all done, how she knew so much about so many things and where she got the energy to do all that she did with such excellence. There wasn't anything she was assigned to do that she didn't get done. There wasn't anything she desired to achieve that she didn't accomplish. It seemed as if she was unstoppable. Sure, she had some disappointments along the way. And yes, there were setbacks and stumbling blocks she encountered, but she *never* gave up and she *never* gave in. She was anchored in the Lord, knew she had a work to do, and she stood on the Word of God. Her favorite scripture was, *"But they that wait upon the Lord, shall renew their strength, they shall mount up on wings as an eagle, they shall run and not be weary, and they shall walk and not faint"* (Isaiah 40:31). With every accomplishment, Arriana would always say: "To God Be the Glory!" She was fearless on the journey!

###

It's 6:30 a.m. on Wednesday, December 27, 2017, and I have finally mustered up the nerve to start writing the book my baby told me to write about her journey. She even gave me the name of the book when she first began her treatment. Her book would be titled, *Fearless on the Journey*.

I remember when it all got started in 2016. Arriana had been feeling extremely tired for weeks in December and January…so weak at times she couldn't walk very far or go up the stairs in her house. Thinking she might be anemic, she went to see her doctor. Tests came back showing Cancer/Leukemia. We were sitting in her room at Northside Hospital's blood and bone marrow treatment area of the Northside cancer treatment division trying to make sense of all the information we had received from her team of doctors. As we talked about the diagnosis from the doctors, we knew her type of Leukemia was very serious. It was the most aggressive type and the one with the lowest survival rate – Acute Myeloid Leukemia (AML). But we disregarded all of the negatives; we were Christians. We believed in the power of our God to heal any disease. We knew our God was a miracle working God, and He would work a miracle for her (us). He would get the glory from Arriana's testimony of her healing. We rebuked and bound up the negative numbers, as well as the low survival rate. We knew none of the negative reports applied to us. Not us – not Rev. Arriana Mills Daniel and Bishop/Pastor Frances V. Mills. Those words were from the enemy, the devil, and we knew his tricks. We were under attack. This was the enemy's way of trying to stop the powerful ministry God had given her. We declared victory, and God would get the glory. We bound the devil and every imp he had sent to attack her; we sent them back to the pits of hell from whence they came – in Jesus' name!

We were very optimistic as she (we) began her treatment. Her team of doctors proceeded with very aggressive treatment – massive doses of chemo immediately for the first 30 days. And then we would see a difference. If not, we had other options; there was hope. Wow! That seems so long ago now. During this time, she said, "God is saying write my testimony, so others can read about how He is going to cure me. He will get the glory."

###

I dreamed about Arriana for the first time after she passed on Monday, October 23, 2017. I think of her every minute. I talk to her each and every day – all day long. I've asked God, "Why?" so many times, I can't put a number to the times. I ask God to speak to me, give me a reason. I ask "Re" (as I have always called her) to please come back and speak to me; let me know she's alright. I want her to come back and show me her beautiful smiling face, one more time, and let me hear her say, "Mommy, I'm okay." But she hasn't revealed herself to me, and God has not answered my "why?"

    I believe my baby is here with me because we made that promise to each other many years ago. We agreed that whoever left this earth first would come back and let the other know she is here. We would do something only we would recognize and know without a doubt the other person is present. At least, today, I dreamed about my baby.

CHAPTER 2

THE BATTLE IS NOT YOURS

And he said, Hearken ye, all Judah, and ye inhabitants of Jerusalem, and thou king Jehoshaphat, Thus saith the LORD unto you, Be not afraid nor dismayed by reason of this great multitude; for the battle is not yours, but God's (2 Chronicles 20:15).

How many times have I made that statement? How often have I quoted that scripture to some unforeseen circumstance that came to throw me off course, to take my mind and focus off what I know God has called me to do? How many times have I told the devil he is a liar, that I didn't have to worry because my God was fighting for me, and all I had to do was "stand still and see the salvation of the Lord"? More times than I can put a number to is my answer. How about you?

It is true; our God brings this scripture to us on many occasions when it looks like we're not going to win. He reminds us: "The battle is not yours; it's the Lord's." So, we rest in it. Hallelujah! God's got it.

The words in the above scripture were the very ones we uttered between our tears on that sad Friday, February 17, 2016, when the doctors came into the emergency room examination area. They were running tests and doing various exams on my daughter, Arriana all day since around 10:30 a.m. They told her they had seen some things in her blood and needed to run more tests. They asked her if anyone in her family had any blood disorders. She had called me to find out if I knew of anyone in the family with such a condition.

Her dad and I were in Augusta, Georgia visiting her dad's oldest brother who was in the hospital and not doing well. Dad wanted to visit his brother one more time before he passed away. The doctors had not given the family much hope according to the information we got from my sister-in-law, his wife.

So, on Thursday morning, Dad and I left to spend a few days in Augusta to see his brother. I knew before we left town that Arriana was not feeling well for several weeks. She was very weak and extremely tired. She complained about having shortness of breath just trying to walk up her stairs at home; she had to sit down to catch her breath about halfway up.

She drove over to the house on Monday to visit her dad and me. When she came through the door, she had to stop and catch her breath. She repeated again that she was out of breath just walking from her car in the driveway into the house. I knew immediately that something was seriously wrong, so I made her sit down and call her doctor for an appointment. I felt she may be anemic, but she thought it was because she was trying to do so much over the holidays and her body needed rest.

She went to see her doctor that Wednesday. He drew blood and sent it off to be tested. She was to call back the next day to get the results. On Thursday morning, she waited until the doctor's office opened at 9:00 a.m. and called to get her results. They told her they didn't receive them yet and asked her to call back before lunch. Dad and I had planned to be on the road by then.

I was so torn. I didn't want to leave my baby to deal with this by herself. I called to let her know I was going to tell Dad we couldn't go to Augusta, but she said, "Absolutely not." Her Daddy needed to see his brother before he passed away. She promised to call me when she got the results, and she knew she would be okay. She figured it was probably just going to show that she was anemic.

Dad and I left for Augusta at 10:30 a.m. We got there around noon and went to visit my sister-in-law at her house first. Then we went to the hospital around 3:00 p.m., but we only stayed for a little while because Dad was exhausted, needed to eat and then rest. At that time, he was still suffering from a stroke he had a few years back. We left the hospital, took my sister-in-law to dinner, and then checked into the hotel. I realized I hadn't heard from Arriana, so I called her. She told me what had transpired from the time she had gotten the results of her blood work from her PCP. Her doctor told her that her blood count was very low. He suggested she see a hematologist who would probably recommend she get some blood.

She immediately started calling various hematologists in her insurance network and none could see her for a month. Only one doctor's office asked her questions about why the rush to see the hematologist. She explained her symptoms and what her PCP had recommended. The nurse asked if she knew what her blood level was and if not, to contact her doctor for the number and call her back. She told her based on that info, she might be able to get her an appointment sooner. Arriana called her PCP and was told the number was 7. When she called back the nurse and told her the count, she told Arriana, "You don't need to see the hematologist; you need to go immediately to the emergency room to get some blood." She instructed Arriana to contact her doctor's office again and have them call the emergency room of the nearest hospital. Her doctor was to notify the hospital he was sending Arriana to get blood immediately and for him to give them her blood count number.

The nurse instructed Arriana that under no circumstances was she to drive. Someone had to drive her to the hospital. By this time, it was almost 4:30 pm and Mitch, Arriana's hubby, would have been home any minute. She decided to wait until he got home to tell him what had transpired and what they needed to do. When Mitch arrived, they talked and decided not to alarm the kids but to wait and go to the hospital the next morning after they got the kids off to school. Once she got her pints of blood, they would probably be back home before the kids got off the school bus.

After talking to Arriana, I was ready to leave and go home to be with my baby. But once again, she convinced me to stay the course and allow Dad to spend time with his brother.

After all, that's what we drove all the way over there for. She reassured me all would be okay. Mitch was going to drive her to the hospital Friday morning, and they would probably be back home within a couple of hours. I reluctantly agreed not to get back on the road as it was late and getting dark. And besides, I didn't get any rest all day either, so I needed a good night's rest.

I prayed that night asking God to take care of my baby and to let everything be okay the next day when she got to the hospital. I asked Him to let her go back home to be with her family. When Dad and I got up that Friday morning, I was very uneasy; I felt a nervous sensation in my stomach. I told Dad about Arriana's situation and that I couldn't stay in Augusta while she was going through whatever it was in her body. I told him I needed to go back home to be with her. Dad agreed. Praise the Lord! He said he was good; he had seen his brother on Thursday and had talked with him. And although his brother was unresponsive, he believed his brother heard what he said.

We packed up and checked out. We went by my sister-in-law's house to tell her what had happened and that we were leaving. She understood and told us she would keep us updated on James' situation. We left Augusta around 11:30 a.m. and arrived home at 1:00 p.m. I dropped Dad off at the house as he had already told me to go on to be with Re (Arriana). He didn't feel strong enough to go with me. He just needed to get in bed and rest.

I called Re once I left the house to see if they were at the hospital or at home. When she answered her phone, she sounded exhausted. I asked what was wrong, and she said they were still at the hospital waiting for the results of the tests they had been running. They hadn't even started to give her the blood. I said, "Okay, I was just checking on you." I made it to the hospital (Piedmont Fayetteville) in 30 minutes when it would normally take, at least, an hour. When I walked into her room back in the emergency area – she just broke down crying on my shoulder. My "fearless" baby was scared. OMG, what is going on? Why is it taking so long? We prayed; we stated with assurance, "This battle is not ours; it's the Lord's!" We refused to receive any negative reports.

Then three doctors and an intern came into the room. They apologized that we had to wait so long but when they drew her blood that morning, they saw some things they didn't like, some things they questioned. As a result, they drew more blood and sent it to an outside lab for deeper analysis. They had to wait for those results, and now, they had them. The tests showed that Arriana had Leukemia. We were all speechless – Arriana, Mitch, and I. We sat there for what seemed like 20 minutes trying to digest what they had said.

Arriana finally asked, "What did you say?" And the doctor repeated it. I think we both spoke at the same time and said, "What does that mean?" The doctor tried to explain, but I don't think it was sinking in for either of us. Tears rolled down Arriana's face and mine. Mitch was holding her as she laid her head on his shoulder. I was just sitting there in disbelief trying not to cry loudly. I heard Arriana ask the question, "Is Leukemia cancer? The doctor responded, "Yes, it is – it's a cancer of the blood." He went on to say, "We are going to admit you to the hospital because we need to put you in a room and start giving you blood. You'll probably get about 5 or 6 pints tonight. In the morning, we will transport you to Northside Hospital's Blood and Bone Marrow Center. They are the best in the SE for treating this type of cancer. We'll transport you by ambulance. Your family can meet you there." They all said their apologies and to let them know if there was anything we needed or that they could do for us.

In about half an hour, they came and rolled my baby up to a room. They began setting up all the machinery and connecting all the tubes for her intravenous treatments to begin. Mitch and I talked. We decided I should stay with Re while he went home to get the kids and pack Arriana a bag. I agreed. Whatever he wanted me to do I was there to do. He wanted to bring the kids back to the hospital, so he and Re could explain what was happening with Mommy. Oh Lord, my babies are so young. How will they – how can they understand this? I uttered in my spirit – Lord, help us! I kept repeating to myself: "This battle is not ours; it's the Lord's."

Mitch sat on the bed with Re after they started the first pint of blood. The doctors came up to check on Re to see if we had any questions and how we were doing. They assured us that Leukemia was treatable and curable and the team at Northside was the best. When they all left, Mitch said, "Let us pray." And we did. We prayed for total, swift healing and strength for us all to get through this. We declared God's Word: "By His stripes, Arriana is healed." We declared and decreed, "The devil is a liar, and he has no authority over us." We declared, "Every Word God has spoken to us is true. We are victorious and more than conquerors through Christ our Lord." We prayed and we prayed. We anointed Arriana's body, and we pleaded the blood of Jesus to cover, heal, and restore her to do everything He created and called her to do – in Jesus' name. Amen. After the prayer, we all felt better. And Mitch left to pick up the kids.

While Mitch was gone, I sat at my baby's bedside and held her hand. Soon, I saw her lips begin to quiver, and the tears started rolling down the side of her face falling into her ears. I got up and held her; we both just cried and cried as she kept saying: "Oh, Mommy, why is this happening to me?" I had no answer; all I could say was: "I don't know baby. I don't know. You've done so much in serving and being obedient to the Lord. He is not punishing you. You've been so good, loving, and kind. You have given so much; only God knows. But I believe God is going to heal this, and you're going to have an awesome testimony."

And thus, on Friday, February 17, 2016, Arriana's journey to her healing began! We declared, "This battle is not ours, but it's the Lord's." And she would say, "This is just part of my journey."

CHAPTER 3

ONE MORE RIVER TO CROSS

The senior choir in our church used to sing a song entitled, "One More River to Cross." Having been the choir director for the Sunbeam choir, the youth choir, the women's choir, and the senior choir, Arriana was very familiar with this song. And for whatever the reason, the title stayed with her. She would be humming the tune or singing a few verses of the song, and I'd ask her why she was singing that. She would always say, "I don't know; it just came to me."

She was an "old soul." People would say that she was an old lady in a young girl's body. She was mature acting and mature thinking all of her life. She always wanted to do the right thing and encouraged others to do the same.

I'll never forget during her senior year in high school when the seniors had planned "Senior Skip Day" (this was a day when they would not show up at school but would meet in a park and have a party). Arriana called me at work that morning and asked me if she could participate. She said she didn't want something to happen, and I might be looking for her at school, and she not be there. Lord, I laughed so hard.

And yes, she got permission from her mama to skip school and go party.

###

One day, we were out shopping, and we saw a painting in an art gallery. The title of it was – you guessed it – "One More River to Cross." She said, "Mom, I've got to have this painting." It was beautiful, absolutely breathtaking. It was a painting of a young woman with outstretched arms and feet leaping over a body of water (a river). Her face was aglow with peace, and joy. All we could do was stare at that painting. Arriana said, "Mom, this painting is me; every time I conquer one challenge, and another is presented to me, this is what I say to myself. This is how I feel."

We checked with the salesperson hoping it was affordable, but the price of the painting was way beyond what we could afford. She was a little sad, but she told the salesperson, "Don't sell my painting. I'll be back." A couple of months later, I walked into her apartment and there it was, hanging in her living room. Wow, what a statement that painting made. And the more I saw the painting, the more I realized the girl in the painting looked like Arriana. Wow! How strange was that?!

So, there we were, Saturday, February 18, 2016, and my baby was lying in a bed in Northside Hospital's Blood and Bone Marrow Center. A team of about 8 to 10 doctors were standing before us talking about an "aggressive treatment plan" for her cancer. She was diagnosed with Acute Myeloid Leukemia (AML), the worst type – the type with the lowest survival rate. But they were hopeful and confident that with an aggressive treatment plan, her story would be different. They could get her into "remission."

My mind went back to her beautiful painting: "Okay, Lord, she has one more river to cross, and we *know* she will cross it too. You've enabled her to cross all the rest. We know you'll do it again."

As we listened to each doctor and the role they would play in her treatment plan, we began to realize how serious the situation really was. It was sinking in. My baby was really in a fight for her life; she had the big "C" – cancer. We were afraid! We were nervous! We didn't know enough to be able to ask a lot of questions; we were still in shock.

I had hoped that the specialists there would determine it was a "misdiagnosis" by the doctors at Piedmont Fayetteville, and we would be told something else. Perhaps, it was a bad case of anemia after all. This could not be happening. Oh, God! How? Why? Where did it come from? How did she get it? Why my baby? We all had a million questions for the doctors. They were very patient with us because we knew nothing about Leukemia. They gave us books and pamphlets to read to get a better understanding of the disease and what to expect as Arriana went through each phase of treatment. They provided us with information on outside resources to call and connect with.

After they left the room, I called my niece who is a nurse; we shared with her what we had just been told. We asked her to find out for us if this was the best hospital for

Arriana's treatment, and if it wasn't, what was the name of the best. It didn't matter where – just the best. We asked her to keep this situation confidential as we were not ready to share it with anyone just yet. When she called back in what seemed like hours but was only about 30 minutes, Shayron (my niece) said MD Anderson in Houston, Texas was known as the best hospital for treating Leukemia and especially, AML. She further stated that Northside was also well known and considered the best in the SE as the doctors at Northside Blood and Bone Marrow Center came out of MD Anderson to start the Center at Northside.

We had a decision to make: do we transfer to MD Anderson or stay at Northside? I was in favor of transferring; Mitch wanted it to be Arriana's decision. She wanted to pray about it overnight, and we all agreed to pray and seek God for direction. The next day when we all gathered in her room, Arriana told us she wanted to stay at Northside. That way, she would still be close to her babies, Mitch, and her family.

The three of us started to put a plan together to make sure the kids were taken care of daily and so that someone would be with Arriana daily as well. We were told the aggressive plan of treatment would probably have her feeling sick, nauseous, and weak. Mitch decided to take time off from work for a while. I offered to stay with Arriana at night, so he could be with Sydney and Christopher. Once they were off to school, he would come to the hospital, and I would go home to check on Dad. Then on weekends, he could stay with Re all weekend, and I would keep the kids.

The aggressive treatments began the very next week. They had tested and tested, drawn blood and given more blood for several days. Finally, by Wednesday, the first massive doses of chemo began. She would have 7 days of 24-hour doses then off for 3 days. Then another round for 5 days and then off for a week. After that, another round for 7 days and so on; this would go on for 30 days. In the beginning, Re did good – no sickness, no nausea. She was in good spirits laughing, talking, and doing "FaceTime" with the kids. I decorated her room with family pictures of her, Mitch, her babies, her dad, Ervin, and me. I put up beautiful plaques with encouraging scriptural quotes and of course, the many, many get well cards that had started to come once word got out that Rev. Arriana Mills Daniel was sick in the hospital, and she had cancer. Her brother Ervin, sisters (not blood but her BFF's – Carla and Paula) and her cousin Shayron were the only visitors allowed. Visitors had to be limited as her immune system was weakening, and she needed to preserve her strength. Each day, all I could say was – "One more river to cross, Lord."

Around the third week, Re wanted to see her babies, and they wanted/needed to see their mommy. We begged her doctors to please let the kids come to visit even if just for a few minutes. They finally agreed and her nurses set it up. They reserved a sterile room; Re had to wear a mask, sterile gown, and coverings on her feet and hands. The kids had to be covered as well; as a matter of fact, we all did. Before Mitch brought them into the room, he prepped them so they would know what to expect when they saw Mommy. But more than that, they had to be told they couldn't touch her because she was so susceptible to germs that would make her sicker.

I don't know how we got through that visit. My baby was so happy to finally see her babies. When they walked in that room, they forgot all about not touching Mommy. They ran straight over to her, and she hugged them too but only briefly. They had so many questions: what are all the tubes for? Why are all those machines connected to her? Why is she covered up like that? And of course, when is Mommy coming home? Re did great. I could see the tears welling up in her eyes, but she managed to keep it together and talked in a very calm but upbeat voice. She asked the kids about school and what was happening with them. She wanted them to still do their best, keep up with their homework and studies, as well as help Daddy around the house.

She told them not to worry about her because the doctors were making her well, and she would be back home soon. But for now, she needed to be at the hospital. She even got them to play some games with her while they were there. This visit was good for them and Re. And then, it was time for the kids to leave. What was only to be a 45-minute visit turned into an hour. The nurses were great; they knew she needed to be with her babies, so they allowed the extended time before they came to take her back to her room. Favor! Thank you, Jesus!

The treatments continued, and Re got weaker. By then, she had lost all of her hair. Well, she didn't really lose it; once it started to come out in clumps, she told the nurse to go ahead and shave it all off. She was still a strong and brave soul – ready to face whatever was coming. "This too was just part of her journey."

Other issues began to occur: kidney, pneumonia, and blood pressure issues. Additional treatments and new medications were tried; it went on and on and on. Re started to show signs of irritability and some depression. She had been in the hospital since February 16, and it was now mid-April. She told the doctors she needed to go home to see her babies if only for a little while. In April, the doctors allowed her to go home. But while at home, she had to be taken to the hospital for treatments and tests every day. We formed a team to be her caregivers and drivers to and from the hospital.

Mitch went back to work in April. He was such a tower of faith, patience, and organization. When Re was in the hospital, his daily schedule consisted of getting Sydney and Chris off to school each morning, going to work, leaving work and going to the hospital, going home, taking care of Sydney and Chris. When Re was allowed to come home, he kept up with her meds, the scheduling of all her doctor's appointments, hospital visits for tests, in-home physical therapists visits, clinic visits, maintained a calendar of kids' activities, helped with their homework, did the laundry, cleaned the house, and maintained the schedule of the caregivers team we put together. And it worked! We didn't miss a beat with care for the kids or for Re. Can I just say: "Teamwork makes the dream work."

Re was at home for about a month but had to be readmitted. She was in and out of the hospital for weeks at a time. Doctors determined that the massive doses of chemo treatments hadn't worked as they had hoped. To stay alive, Re would need a bone marrow transplant. Ervin her brother volunteered immediately. But the doctors said he probably would not be a good match, so they began the search for a donor. There was no match in the national donor bank. Dad and I were ruled out, but they decided to test Ervin, her brother. He was a match! Hallelujah! Okay, Lord: "One more river to cross!"

The bone marrow transplant was scheduled for June. Near the end of May, they placed Re in the hospital for more rounds of "aggressive and massive" doses of chemo to get her ready for the transplant. Ervin too had to undergo a month of treatments to prepare his body for being a donor. How we all prayed. "Lord, please let this work." My baby was very sick and weak by now. She couldn't eat very much and had lost quite a bit of weight. But she never complained; she never got angry. She would always say: "This is just part of my journey."

June 23, 2016 was the day for the bone marrow transplant surgery. The entire family was at the hospital: Mitch, Dad, Keisha (Ervin's wife), Ervin's 3 oldest children, and me. Ervin's procedure was first. They connected him to the machine that would draw his blood out, separate the bone marrow/stem cells and deposit it into a bag or several bags as it was collected. Then they returned his blood to his body. Before they began his procedure, Re asked if she could see her brother. The nurses covered her in a sterile mask, gown, and other coverings, and wheeled her across the hall to see her brother. When she got to him, they both hugged and cried. She told him thanks for what he was doing to save her life. By that time, we were all in tears. Somebody took a picture of the two of them hugging – what a beautiful picture of pure love! Thank you, son. You gave your sister one more year to enjoy life. You are my hero!

The bone marrow surgery was a success! Hallelujah! Re had to remain in the hospital for another month to continue being monitored. They had to make sure her body was not rejecting the new bone marrow. The meds were strong; she was sick and weak. Again, numerous medical issues arose. The doctors said they were common after a transplant but treatable. After a while, we started to see improvement. The doctors agreed to let Re go home to recuperate. However, she had to be totally isolated from the outside world. No visitors other than immediate family were allowed. She had to make daily visits to the hospital to be monitored and receive intravenous meds, as well as fluids. We could do that.

I became the primary caregiver. The team was back in place, but I took responsibility for the primary care of the kids and Re. Mitch went back to work. I would go over to their house by 6:00 a.m. each morning, get the kids up and ready for school and take them to the bus stop. Then I would go back to the house to get Re up, ready to eat breakfast, and take meds or head to the hospital for meds, fluids, and doctor visits. We had a well-oiled, well-run machine. I enjoyed being there taking care of my baby. And my grans. Thank you, Jesus, that I retired when I did. You knew I would need to be available for this part of the journey.

By October, we started to see great improvement. Trips to the hospital for monitoring were reduced to 2 or 3 times a week. Re's numbers were improving. She was getting better and stronger. She was able to get out of the house for short periods of time but still had to be careful. She couldn't be around a lot of people and could not eat at restaurants. By February 2017, her doctors said she was in remission. Hallelujah! Glory to God!

We shouted and praised God for His marvelous works! Re returned to church in February. We were still being careful. She always wore a mask when out and around people. The church went crazy the Sunday she showed up. She still had to be checked and monitored at the hospital but only a few times a month. All was going well. She began her service to the Lord once again: directing the choir, teaching children's church, preaching the gospel. We even planned our annual summer trip to the beach where we take all the grandkids, nieces, and nephews for a week at Tybee Island. We asked her doctors for permission for Re to go, and they said yes. OMG! She can go. Re can really go to the beach again! So, the last week of June, we were off to the beach for 7 days. We had reserved 2 condos. We had to travel in 3 cars to get everyone, all the boogie boards, beach items, and pool toys down there. We made it safely and had the time of our lives – Re, Dad, Keisha, D'Andria (my niece and Re's little sister), 7 children ages 7 to 13 (3 boys/4 girls) and I. We all had a ball. I'll never ever forget that vacation. What memories. Looking back, it was as if God made this one different, more exciting, more fun-filled, more laughter – so special because it would be our last one with Re.

In July, Re and Mitch took Sydney and Chris on their family vacation. The doctor's said she was good to go – doing fine. So off they went on another trip. They too had a ball. Life was good again. But in August, Re started to feel tired. The doctors said she should return to the hospital to be tested on a weekly basis. They changed some of her meds and the monitoring started again. By September, she was having problems breathing and her appetite was decreasing. She said the meds killed her taste buds and made the food taste funny. The doctors put her on several inhalers to help her breathing. But it got worse. She was getting weaker. By mid-September, she had to use a walker to help steady her steps and keep her from falling. At home, she moved to the downstairs bedroom, so she would not have to go up and down the stairs. I went over every day to help out: getting the kids to school and taking care of Re. "Oh Lord, please help my baby! What's going wrong in her little body?

By October, my baby couldn't walk or stand on her own. Mitch got her a wheelchair. She had to go to the hospital for treatments every other day. I had to bathe my baby, dress her, pick her up, put her in her wheelchair and carry her to the doctors when she had her appointments.

On Monday, October 16, 2017, Mitch took the day off to take her to her doctor's appointment. He called me and Dad and said the doctors wanted to admit Re that day to run tests to see what was causing the paralysis, but she refused to be admitted. I told him to bring her home, and we would come to the house and talk to her.

When we got there, Mitch had gotten her into bed. I went in to talk to Re. I asked why she didn't want to let the doctors find out what was wrong. She replied she was tired of hospitals and didn't want to go back another time. She said the doctors could run their tests on an outpatient basis. Mitch said the doctors had stated the kind of tests they needed to do would require Re's admission to the hospital for a few days, then she could go home. So, I begged her to please go and let the doctors do the tests. That way, they could start whatever treatments necessary to get her walking again. She cried so hard, and I just held her in my arms as she said, "Mommy, I don't want to go back to the hospital, but I'll go." The next day, Mitch took her back to Northside Blood and Bone Marrow Center. On Wednesday, they did a spinal tap. On Wednesday evening, the doctors came and talked to Mitch and me. The spinal tap showed cancer had come back; this time, it was in Re's spine. They would begin aggressive chemo treatments immediately: injections of chemo into her spine. Her first treatment would be the next day – Thursday.

Oh, no Lord, please no! Not again! How did it come back? Why did it come back? I had so many questions. Plan B – can we move Re to MD Anderson now? Her doctors said it was too dangerous, but we could try if we desired to. I was desperate. I called a cousin who is a doctor here in Atlanta and asked if he could help us get Re into MD Anderson. My cousin got us a contact with MD Anderson. Mitch and I called him and inquired about the possibility of moving Re to MD Anderson. The answer was hard to hear; they couldn't receive her in the condition she was currently in. Back to Plan A.

On Thursday, October 17, they performed the first injection of chemo into Re's spine. She was heavily sedated and didn't start recovering from the anesthesia until around 4 o'clock. Mitch was with her all day and night since they admitted her on the Tuesday. I went the Thursday morning right after they had taken her down for the treatment. We were both there when she started to come around. I tried to get her to eat, but she wasn't ready. She was thirsty, and I gave her water. She took a few sips and went back to sleep. Mitch told me he was going for a walk. I stayed with Re, and I prayed and cried and prayed and cried. When she woke up again, Mitch was back, and he tried to get her to eat. She took a few bites of her dinner. My baby looked so weak and helpless. Oh, God, help my baby!

I sat with Mitch and Re until about 9:30 p.m., and I told them I was going to leave to check on Dad, but I would be back early the next day. I gave Re a kiss and told her good night. She was in and out of sleep only saying a few words each time – still recovering from the anesthesia. She opened her eyes as I stood by her bed, and she reached for my hand. I held her little hand so bruised from all the needle sticks. She looked up at me and smiled. She said, "Mommy, I love you." And I said to her, "I love you too baby." I was fighting back the tears. My baby was so sick. She looked me in the eyes and said, "Mommy, thank you for everything you've done for me." And I quickly responded, "Oh, baby, this is just what Mommies do for their babies." I told her to get some rest, and I would see her in the morning. She smiled and nodded.

Those were the last words my baby ever spoke to me. I'll never ever forget her little voice and the expression on her face. I know now that she was telling me goodbye. I hugged Mitch and told him, "See you in the morning son."

Friday morning, 12:30 a.m. my cell phone rang. It shook me out of a deep sleep. I looked at it, and I saw Mitch's name.

OMG! Something has happened to Re. I said, "Hi son." And he said, "Mom, I just want you to know Re is having some breathing problems. The doctors are moving her to ICU to put her on a breathing machine to help her breathe easier."

I asked, "Do I need to come down there?"

He said, "No, "I'll get all of her things out of the room, and they'll get her moved. I'll call if anything changes." I said, "Okay, but I'll be there first thing in the morning as soon as I get Dad settled."

The next morning, I walked down the hall to ICU, talking to the Lord and tearing up on the inside – again. I had cried all the way to the hospital. I said, "Lord, help me when I get to see my baby." ICU – Intensive Care Unit, what does all this mean?

When I got to her room, I walked in, hugged Mitch and asked, "How is she?" He said she was about the same. The doctors said the machine was only breathing about 40% for her; she was doing the rest. They didn't know what caused the breathing issues, but they were running tests. I went over to my baby, and I could see her eyes moving under her eyelids. I began talking to her, "Hi baby, I hope you can hear me. I believe you can because I see your eyes moving. You're going to be alright. Hold on, keep on fighting. We love you, baby." I took her cell phone, and turned to Pandora, so she could listen to gospel music. She always did that when she was in the hospital before

Friday went by, and there was no change. The doctors said she would get her second chemo injection on Monday.

Mitch and I decided that I should stay with her on Sunday night, and then he would go home to be with the kids. I asked him if he thought they might want to come to see Re over the weekend. He said he would ask them. On Saturday, all of Mitch's sisters came up from Ala to see Re. We took turns going back to ICU. Sunday evening, I went to the hospital to relieve Mitch. He said the kids didn't want to see their mommy the way she was. He went home to be with them.

All night, the nurses and doctors came in and out checking Re, administering meds, and making notes on her chart. I asked how she was doing, and they said her vitals looked good. By morning, the shift changed, and the nurse said they would soon come to take Re for her second chemo injection. I said okay, I would wait until they came and then I would leave. By that time, Mitch would be there.

9 o'clock came, 9:30, then 10:00 a.m. I asked the nurse if they were still coming to get Re. She said she would check on it as they should have done so by now. At 10:15 a.m., I decided to leave so that I could get home to take Dad to his 1:00 p.m. doctor's appointment. Mitch had called to say he was on the way. I told the nurse and I left.

On I-285 approaching Memorial drive exit at 11:00 a.m. My phone rang. It was Mitch. "Hi Mom, have you left the hospital?" I said, "Yes son, what's up?" The hospital had just called him to say something had happened to Re, and we needed to get there in a hurry. He said he was on the way but struggling through downtown traffic. I told him I would turn around and head back. I asked him if he wanted me to wait on him before I went in. He said no.

I raced back to the hospital – praying and crying out to God to help my baby. "Please God." When I got to her room, the curtains were drawn, and the doctor met me as I slowly opened the door. He stopped me from going in. He said Re's heart had stopped beating, and they had to resuscitate her. Her heart rate kept dropping; they were working to get it back up and stable. He cautioned me that when I entered the room, I would see a lot of blood around her because they had not gotten a chance to clean her up yet. They were just trying to keep her stable.

When I stepped into the room, I almost passed out. Re was not covered. Blood was everywhere: on the floor around her bed, on her bed, and on her gown. The machine was doing all the breathing. She was lifeless. Her eyes weren't moving any longer. I couldn't get close to her because there were many doctors and nurses doing all sorts of things to her.

I just sat on the side crying and praying. Was this really happening? I felt as if I was dreaming. Why was it happening? Re was supposed to be getting better. God was supposed to be working a miracle for her, for us. We prayed for it. We know He can; our faith was unshakable. We were still believing – God is able. He was going to show up right away. I cried, "Turn this situation around, Lord. Show Yourself mighty in this room. Let Re have her testimony about how You healed and delivered!"

Mitch showed up, and the doctors told him the same things they told me. He was solemn, quiet, and teary-eyed. My poor son-in-law, he was steadfast and unmovable in his faith too. He was strong in supporting and helping his little wife through all of this. He looked so sad as he sat beside me. I put my arms around him as we sat in silence watching the nurses and doctors do their thing.

Finally, about 2:30 p.m. the doctor came over to talk to us and give us an update. He said they had done all they could and gave all the meds they could, but nothing was keeping her heart rate up. It kept dropping. He asked if Re's heart stopped again if we wanted them to resuscitate again? Mitch looked at me and said no. I nodded in agreement. The nurse walked over and touched the doctor; she shook her head. The doctor looked at us and said, "She's gone." Oh no God, my baby is gone. How can this be? Why did You let her leave us? Oh God! Oh God! Oh God!

This was just part of her journey! My baby has crossed her last river!

CHAPTER 4

WHERE DO WE GO FROM HERE?

On Monday, October 23, 2017, the world lost an awesome mother, wife, daughter, sister, auntie, friend to many, female professional, entrepreneur and servant of the Most High God! Rev. Arriana Letrecia Mills Daniel crossed over from Earth to eternity to occupy her heavenly home.

There was so much to do. We were in shock, but we had to take care of business. Mitch and I began calling family members to tell them Re had passed. I called my son Ervin and told him first. I asked him to go to the house and get Dad. I didn't want to tell Dad until his son was there with him. He brought him to the hospital. I called Ervin's (my husband) sister and brother in Waycross. I called my sisters and my brother. My baby sister called her daughter, my niece D'Andria who worked only a few blocks from the hospital. We called Trimble's Mortuary to come and get her body. I called my best friend Karen. I called Re's BFF's / her sisters – Carla and Paula. And I called my pastor, Dr. William Flippin and my friend Bishop Ruth Smith. Mitch called his sister Mittie and asked her to pick up Sydney and Chris and bring them to the hospital. He would tell them what happened to Mommy when they got there. He called his brother George who lives here in Atlanta.

Before long, we had many of our relatives and closest friends there with us at the hospital as we waited for Trimble's Mortuary to come. When Trimble got there, I went over to kiss my baby again, and her little body was cold. No life, no warm blood was running through her. She looked like she was asleep. This was so hard. I could not believe it was real. I knew I was going to wake up from the nightmare – soon. Please God, let me wake up from the nightmare.

Trimble Mortuary told us to come the next day to begin planning the service. They gave us a 10:00 a.m. appointment. We all left the hospital in tears leaning on one another. Mitch took the kids home. Dad, my family and I went to my house. By the time we got there, word had spread fast. Cars and people were everywhere waiting for us to get home. I thank God for loving friends and family who come to see about your well-being in times like these.

In about an hour, Pastor Flippin and Mrs. Flippin came. Wow, he had such a busy schedule, but there he was. They came to comfort me. Pastor Flippin told me not to hesitate to ask him for any assistance I needed. I told him I truly appreciated it and that we may want to hold her service at Greater Piney Grove since my church could not accommodate all of my family, Mitch's family and the people who knew Re and us. He said just let the church know and it was ours.

The days after Re passed, I went through the motions of helping my son-in-law make preparations for her homegoing celebration. Mitch, his sister Mittie, my son Ervin and I worked as a team to get everything done. Mitch didn't want it to drag on; he wanted the kids to try to get on with life. The wake and musical tribute would be held at our church, Tabernacle of Faith where Re was the assistant pastor, and I served as pastor. It would be held on the Thursday night, October 26th (my 70th birthday) and the homegoing would be on Friday, the 27th at Greater Piney Grove Baptist Church where she had grown up and gotten saved. We chose her burial place to be in the same spot where Dad and I picked out our burial plots – near the edge of the lake at Forrest Lawn Memorial Gardens. We met with the mortuary staff on Tuesday morning and then went to Forrest Lawn that afternoon. I went shopping for Re's clothing, while Mitch and Mittie started to work on the program. Carla went with me to pick out my baby's outfit. Money was no object on this. I bought a gorgeous, gold, satin and silk dress, as well as diamond and gold jewelry. Her casket was crème and gold. She was beautiful!

After the service, I was in a fog for weeks. I couldn't eat or sleep and didn't want to be bothered by anyone. I was mad at God. Where do I go from here? Nothing I believed in worked! Prayer didn't work. Unwavering faith didn't work. Fasting and praying didn't work. Where was God and why was He so cruel? How could I preach something I didn't believe in anymore? How could I pray for people who are lost, depressed, and sick – when it didn't work for my baby.

I couldn't stop crying day in and day out – that's all I did. People called, but I didn't want to talk to anyone. I miss my baby. I just wanted to see her one more time, hear her voice one more time and have her tell me she is okay.

Thanksgiving was near, how would I cope without her? Everybody was so used to coming to the house for the big dinner. I couldn't do it. My baby wasn't going to be there. I told Dad I wanted to go away, and he said okay. We headed back to Tybee where I knew I always got direction and heard God speak to me – at the ocean. And besides, that was the place where Re and I had spent the most wonderfully relaxing and fun time just a few months prior. I needed to go back there.

Once again, I had my quiet time walking and sitting on the beach crying out to God. I needed to hear from Him. And just like God – when we cry out to Him, He will answer. I heard God speak. Not only that, but He showed up and revealed Himself to me. Nobody but God would do that for me. He spoke, and I listened. He gave direction, and I accepted. He brought me back from my "dark" place. He renewed my life, my faith, and my trust in Him. He helped me understand that He had a reason for taking my baby, and I'll understand it better by and by. I don't understand it right now, but He will reveal it to me later. He told me to wait on Him. But in the meantime – I have to keep serving Him. I have to keep on being who He created me to be. I have to continue her "legacy."

The question is, "Where do I go from here?" The answer is clear – I go to Him! I remain obedient to Him; I don't belong to myself; I belong to God. Just like He reminded me that Re didn't belong to me. He had only loaned her to me for 50 years. She really belonged to Him all the time. She did what He sent her on the earth to do. And when her assignment was up, and she had accomplished all He sent her to do – He called her home to be with Him once again. Just like Jesus. Wow!

Where do I go from here? Wherever He sends me. Where did Re go from here? Back to her heavenly home!

Where do we all go from here? We each answer that question by the way we live our lives here on earth. Have you accepted Him as Lord and Savior? Have you surrendered your life to Him? Only time will tell. I hope to see you on the other side. After we cross that "last river"…after we travel the last mile of the way!! I pray you and I will also be *Fearless on the Journey.*

CHAPTER 5

LAST PART OF THE JOURNEY
THE VISITS

Visit #1

It's Tuesday, January 9, 2018, and it has been a good day. I have decided to take up the mantle that Arriana started when she was active – volunteering at the kids' schools. I signed up at Sydney and Christopher's schools as a volunteer. So, Tuesday, January 9th was my first day volunteering at Sydney's school, and we were scheduled to sit and have lunch, joined by all of Sydney's BFF's. What a great time I had with my grandbaby. And Sydney was absolutely ecstatic.

My prayers are different now. I still cry a lot, but I pray for Re to visit me, show herself to me or just make herself known to be with me. On my way home from visiting Sydney and volunteering at the school, I stopped by the grocery store to get groceries. I decided to back into the garage to make it easier to get the groceries out and into the house.

As I pulled up to the house, the garage door went up before I could touch my opener. I was in shock. Maybe Ervin

Sr. had gotten up and opened the garage for me. As I backed into the garage, I realized I was getting a little close to the left side of the entrance, so I drove back out and started to back in again. As I was backing in and looking over my right shoulder, I heard a sharp, hard knock on the rear driver side window of the car. I thought someone must have been in the garage, so I stopped and looked around. I didn't see anyone. I stopped the car and looked all around in my rear-view mirror and side mirrors, but I still didn't see anyone. I continued to reverse.

When I got out of the car. I looked around in the garage and no one was there. But someone knocked on the car window. I smiled. Okay, Ms. Arriana that was you. I smiled and said, "Thank you, baby, for letting me know you're here." When I got into the house, Ervin was still in bed asleep. He didn't open the garage. I smiled again. Re, it was you. Thank you, baby, for the visit. I love you girl!

Visit #2

On a cold morning in February 2018, I was sitting in the den reading my scriptures and the Daily Bread. The fireplace was going, and the room was warm and comfortable. All of a sudden, I felt a slight breeze. I looked up, and the ceiling fan was turning. How did that happen? I turned to look at the wall switch; it was not flipped up to turn on the ceiling fan. I looked at it for about a minute, and it was still turning. I smiled.

I remember Re and I had always said that whoever died first would come back to visit the other person and would do something so out of the ordinary we would know it was the person who had passed visiting. I looked up, smiled, and said:

"Thanks baby, for letting me know you're here. The fan stopped turning, and I went back to reading my Bible. In a few minutes, it started turning again. OMG, it was really my baby; she was right there with me. I stopped and with a big smile on my face started talking to Re. I told her I missed her so much and thanks for coming to see about me. The fan stopped turning, and it has never happened again.

Visit #3

June 1, 2018, I woke up and headed downstairs to the kitchen to put the Keurig on for my morning coffee. Re and I would always call each other and start our Keurigs about the same time each morning – 7:00 a.m. While we did that and made ourselves some breakfast, we talked on the phone. We made our coffee and then sat down to watch our favorite morning show "Good Morning America."

On this first day of June when I got to the kitchen, I found the Keurig was already on. I thought I did not turn it off the day before. But even if I didn't, it should have cut itself off automatically. Why didn't it? I decided I would make sure I shut it off that night before I went to bed. I forgot to do so, and when I woke up the next morning, again, the Keurig was already on. It was weird. Again, I decided I would definitely remember to turn it off before going to bed. I did – it was already off when I went into the kitchen before going to bed.

The next morning, I got up, went down to the kitchen to put the Keurig on for coffee and again, it was already on! "What is going on?" I asked myself. "Could it be Re again?" Yes, it was. Every morning for the entire month of June, the

Keurig was already on when I went down to make my coffee. So, I would smile each morning and say, "Thank you, baby." Re was letting me know she was still with me.

Visit #4

I awoke in the middle of the night to the smell of Re's perfume. I sat up in bed and looked around, but I saw no one. Wow, the smell of the perfume was right by my bedside. I looked for Re hoping I would see her in the room, but I didn't. Nevertheless, it was okay. I knew she was there with me.

"Thank you, baby, for continuing to visit your mama. One day, I pray you will reveal yourself to me. I know you feel I can't handle it, but I do believe it will happen one day. Until then, keep on visiting me whenever and however you want to. I love you girl!"

The journey on this side has ended, but my baby's journey isn't really over. The final chapter of her life on earth is over; yet, the memories remain. The legacy continues, but the journey isn't over. It continues. New chapters are being written that I don't know of yet. I must wait until I get to heaven to see what happens next on "The Journey."

In closing, I leave these words with you, my readers:

To Know the will of God is the greatest Knowledge;
To Find the will of God is the greatest Discovery;
To Do the will of God is the greatest Achievement!

                                            (Author Unknown)

Rev. Arriana Letrecia Mills Daniel is still on her journey *doing* the will of God in heaven.

TO GOD BE THE GLORY!

PART 2

Sisters' Reflections of the Journey

CHAPTER 6

REFLECTION – SHAYRON BROWN

Arriana......... Where are you?

I asked her this question, not because I didn't know, but because I couldn't think of anything else to say to mask my racing heartbeat after she told me the lab values.

Ari was like a sister to me. Although we had not spent as much time together in our adult lives as we did as children, we had a bond that was natural, supportive, genuine, and necessary. She always had a very sweet, approachable spirit, and was never too busy to catch up after time had passed without us talking.

I did not find it odd when she called me with a medical question; most of my family does. When I saw her name and number come up, I smiled. I had watched her recent birthday celebration on Facebook. I beamed at every picture of how happy and vibrant she looked – hair salon stop, nail shop stop, lunch with Sydney, I believe, out with the family for dinner, then hot date night with Mitch. Every post was so full of life.

I figured she had a quick question or something to update me on. We exchanged the usual pleasantries asking about each other's families and our parents. Then Ari said, "My doctor wants me to go to the hospital to get a blood transfusion."

"For what?" I asked.

She explained she had a physical a week or so earlier and received a call that her blood count was low. The doctor wanted her to get a transfusion right away.

We talked about how crazy that sounded. The doctor hadn't called her; one of the staff did. She told me the person who called said she should go today. With my nurse brain, I asked casually, "Are you tired, weak, short of breath or dizzy?" Her reply was not at all. She mentioned being tired because of her birthday shenanigans, normal stuff.

Then she said something that made me stop working and listen. "I've been having pain in my legs and lower back... my legs hurt all the time." I asked her what the doctor said, and she responded, "Nothing really." She said he just took some blood during her physical, and she received the call today.

I said call the doctors' office back and ask how low your blood count is. I was curious more than worried. She looked and sounded great. I detected no shortness of breath or labored breathing at all; she just sounded as if she had been doing too much. A while passed, and she called back and gave me the H/H results. I had told her to ask specifically for her hemoglobin and hematocrit count. The numbers she gave me were extremely low – she could pass out any minute low. So, I asked, "Where are you?"

She again confirmed she was home. She was getting ready to pick up one of the kids from school. I calmly told her that was not a good idea because her count was extremely low, and I thought it was dangerous for her to drive. She reassured me she would wait for Mitch.

We talked about her frustration with the internist. She had trusted this person and had been a long-term patient. She was not pleased with how all of this had gone down – neither was I. I couldn't believe an MD whom she had been driving over an hour to see for years didn't call sooner and personally express his concern.

My concern was maybe she had fibroids; that's why her counts were so low. It crossed my mind but not for long. This was a quick fix: get the transfusions, rest, take iron, and she would be fine. We chatted a bit longer; she needed to update Mitch. I asked her to call me back and update me after the transfusions. She promised she would. I believe it was Thursday.

As a kid, Arriana was very creative. We played "make believe" all the time, dressing up our dolls, building playhouses out of blankets and pillows. We played a game while riding in the car. She had a fascination with Station Wagons; of all the cars, she wanted a station wagon – full of kids. I mean every time she saw one, she would squeal, "That's my car." Nobody else would call it because only Arriana wanted a station wagon.

Ari was the nurturer of the group of cousins, concerned about everybody's feelings. She made sure everybody had a turn but also ensured she went first too. She was never unkind to anybody. I don't think she had "bad teenage years." Her spirit was always the same.

Saturday's call from Auntie stopped me in my track, I could instantly make out she was and had been crying hard. Her words were, "Shayron, my baby, my baby has Leukemia. They say she has cancer, and she is being moved to Northside Hospital to start treatment." I didn't process what she was saying; it could not be true. I was thinking a 49-year-old vibrant, strong, woman who looks as amazing as she does, with no real complaints could not have cancer.

I spoke with Ari several days later; she was her normal self, in good spirits, positive, and upbeat. She asked me what I knew about NSH and their Cancer Center. She spoke briefly about her internal medicine doctor and how disappointed she was with him, having been a long-term patient. I told her I would ask around about Northside's reputation.

I spoke with Gerri, a seasoned oncology nurse at work. She confirmed as did several others, Northside's program was top-notch with a very experienced oncologist. Several of our Piedmont patients were referred to Northside. I gave that report to Arianna and Mitch. They seemed at peace, approaching her treatments as a situation to face head-on and get it over with.

I knew she had several rounds/treatments. I was sending text messages of encouragement and leaving voice messages letting her know how the prayers were going up on her behalf, and I knew she was a strong soldier for the Lord. I professed my faith that she was healed over and over to her.

We all worried about how the children and Mitch were doing. I knew my auntie was putting up a strong face; their bond was phenomenal as far back as I could remember.

Ari's room was like that of a princess, very girlie. She had ruffled pink curtains and white furniture. She was the apple of her family's eye. She was always an entertainer, never afraid to stand up and dance, sing or act silly, not a shy kid, just fun loving. We spent many weekends together as kids, "sleepovers" we called them. During the summer, our fathers (brothers) would take us on their "fishing trips." We would pack up in the car, drive to a remote fishing lake/creek and be there all day. We were adventuresome, finding things to do, making caves, playing with the bait, making our famous mud pies. We'd find various "berries" for ingredients, take care to mix the mud and water and pat them out oh so carefully.

Ari and Mitch called me after her second round did not change her numbers. They asked me about the Cancer Center of America. I felt helpless. I wasn't familiar with it; they wanted to get a second opinion. I surely didn't want to give them any bad advice. They seemed shocked the results were not favorable. I asked God why someone like Ari would have to endure such a horrible disease. The words "strong soldier" are what I heard back. Okay, God, you are using her to bless somebody else, but she is already healed. I prayed they would both have the strength to endure. I remembered her message the last time I heard her preach "Distractions," she said from her own mouth, "The enemy doesn't want us to focus on what God has called us to do." She was preaching from her heart with no shoes on…go girl!

I had to see her; my nurse eyes needed to see how things were going wither treatments. I called and asked if she wanted some ice cream. She mentioned she did not have a taste for anything, or she could not taste anything. I went over for lunch. As I put on the reverse isolation coverings, I was thinking of how she would preach this testimony. She was in good spirits and ate a bit of the ice cream. I found the patient refrigerator and labeled the rest of it for her. She could finish it later. Her room was set up like an office; it was so organized. Arriana was sitting up on her chair projecting confidence and the determination to get it finished. She had to get home to the kids.

I was there only a little while before the PA came in. I got up to leave, but she asked me to stay. He introduced himself politely and was very professional. He discussed her biopsy procedure. Her disposition changed. She looked him in the face and expressed how uncomfortable it had been and that she would not do it again. He told her that the lead MD of the group preferred the method and how effective it was. Arriana adjusted herself in the bed where she had moved to for him to examine her. She spoke slowly and firmly, "I will not go through that again." He was caught off guard, smiled a bit, and reassured her he understood. She said in a very dainty way, "Good, I hope so because what we are not going to do is go through that again." She had always been accommodating and flexible as a kid. I laughed to myself – she had a little of me in her – after all.

I cannot imagine what she was going through. Treatment after treatment, staying strong for the kids, for Mitch, for Auntie for everybody. She was not allowed visitors. It seemed time would speed up. I sent text messages whenever I heard a song, a message or when the Holy Spirit led me to send her encouragement. So many people were standing in the gap for her. Her suffering would not be in vain. Finally, the word "remission" was spoken, no cancer cells.

There was another hospital admission for the residual effects of her treatments. Other systems were being challenged. I knew as an RN this was not unusual. These other issues were only "distractions." Arriana had always been a strong soldier; she was fierce and determined. God had spoken that she was already healed.

I visited her again during her hospital stay. I did not call this time; I just went with the Holy Spirit. When I arrived, Mitch was there. He looked surprised and relieved at the same time. She was weaker, apparent signs of a tough battle, but she was still holding on. He was gracious; he did not send me away. Arriana was not feeling well. Mitch needed to leave to get the kids on time, and I was grateful to be able to stay until Auntie made it. Laying in the bed obviously weaker, she talked, and I listened.

Arriana wanted to go home. The kids needed her. She shared the get-well cards they had made for her. She kept saying, "They need me. I need to be at home with them." She laughed at Sydney who was "milking" the extra attention from her teachers. She breathed slowly as she described how Chris wanted to be strong for her. He had turned away so she would not see him cry. She was so proud of both of them. She wanted to go home. There was some discussion that she could go home if she continued to progress.

An attendant from food services came in and took her order. Auntie had shared she was tired of eating the same old thing, and they had been working with her to ensure she got what she wanted. Auntie arrived flustered; the traffic was bad as she came from across town. We stayed with Arriana for a while, and the food was delivered. It was not what she ordered. I could see the disgust on her face. I believe there was some conversation with administration about her food. Auntie called downstairs; next thing I knew, a supervisor was there apologizing profusely, personally taking her meal order, and assuring them they would get it right.

Within a short period, two food trays were delivered to them, hot, appetizing and with very heavy portions. I marveled at the quick turnaround from a nursing perspective. I left that visit thinking, she is no longer going along, no longer accommodating, no longer willing to sacrifice herself. She was fighting for her life, and she was present, attentive to every detail. She knew what meds were due, what time, the dose, and what was to follow. She knew the standards of the hospital and who to call to get her concerns addressed. It appeared as if she did not mind calling. I could tell she now had her "game face" on.

Arriana got to go home. Yes, she was a bit weak but home. She could not hug and kiss, but she was home. She could not go back to church just yet, but she was home!

A year later, she celebrated her birthday. I believe she was in remission. With a new awareness, she seemed determined to live on purpose. She was out on a date night, per Facebook. "How awesome is this?" I said. We spoke; she was still going to the hospital to get antibiotics. What a tremendous sacrifice in order to be at home with her kids. She expressed her gratitude to Mitch for the awesome job he was doing. Of course, she was very thankful to her mom (Auntie).

She looked stronger in every Facebook post; her new hair was very flattering. She made it back to church looking gorgeous. I saw her celebration of their wedding anniversary on Facebook and was grateful she was getting her life back. She had the opportunity to go to her class reunion. I saw on FB that the church was doing a community giveaway. I went there on my way home and found her working very hard trying to bless others by giving away food. She was determined to get back home to prepare for another class reunion event. Mitch was going with her.

Sydney was so happy; she was bouncing around, not too far from Ari. My sister came by and spent a few minutes catching up. We all had things to do that evening. It seemed to be so all the time. We did not spend much time together but made the most of the time we did.

I remember the countless times we spent the night together as kids playing with our Barbie dolls, using our Easy

Bake ovens, going to cheerleading practice at the park, and baton twirling lessons. All those fun times had built an unbreakable bond, no matter how much time we spent or did not spend.

Arriana was an entertainer, leader, and counselor all her life. She coordinated the backyard choir of 1211 Thomas Street every summer. At the end of a long, hot, summer day playing with our Waycross friends or an evening on the porch with Grandma shelling peas, snapping beans or hulling corn from the large Crocker sacks, the night ended the same way. We all gathered on the back steps to have our piece of cold watermelon with sprinkles of salt; then it would be time for the talent show.

Arriana would assign the songs, who would sing the songs, and what we would sing together, and we all followed along. We only knew one or two songs, "We are Family" (Sister Sledge) and "Lean on Me" (Otis Redding). We would sing, and she would definitely be the lead with her beautiful voice even back then. She always seemed to know exactly what to do.

I saw something on social media; I think it was National Sibling Day, and Ari was thanking her brother for her bone marrow transplant. I saw pictures of the class reunion party she attended. My summer was going by very quickly, and then I heard she had a bad infection. We talked one morning on my way to work. She was trying to be chipper. I could sense she was growing weary. She said the kids were fine and that she was reserving her energy. She did not want to go back to the hospital. She was making daily trips. I wanted her to feel better. I shared a song that made me think of her, "You Will

Live." Our conversation was brief. I had not seen her since June; she seemed to be on her way back to a full recovery. She was pushing herself; the infection was just a "distraction."

I continued to get updates from Auntie. She was dealing with the infection. Auntie shared there were times she just did not want to talk. In my "RN brain," I was struggling with why the infection was not clearing up. I did not know the details. I was processing that something else had to be going on. Though I am not an oncology RN, I felt as if there had to be another option to give her some relief.

The prayers continued. I asked my deaconess board to pray. I called her name on the weekly intercessory prayer call, and we asked God to restore Arriana. She did not deserve this. Many questions troubled my mind, and I asked God how and why He allowed it to happen to Arriana. His response to me was that she is His strong soldier, and He needed her life testimony to show others how to truly worship Him. I did not know she was still participating in prayer, Sunday school, and Bible study herself. I heard Bishop Ruth Smith later say this at her musical tribute. I was not surprised; God's words came back to me.

It was the first Saturday in October after the cancer walk at my church. I was thinking of both my cousins who were fighting this dreadful disease. I had not heard either of their voices in a while. I communicated via text. Sometimes they responded; sometimes they did not. I left voice messages; I wanted to hear their voices. That Saturday, they both answered the phone. I had great conversations with them.

My conversation with Arriana was different; she sounded resolved. The effort to sound positive was not there. She was matter of fact. She was tired; she spoke slowly and was deliberate with her words. We talked about how she had to get better. She said it over and over. I have got to get better. Her major concern was Auntie. She said, "My mom is almost 70 years old." I had to stop and think; wow, our parents are aging. I made a joke. I told her, "You know your mom is a superhero; she has the energy of a 25-year-old." She did not laugh. She kept saying it was too much for her momma.

She said she had Grandma to deal with. We talked briefly about her mother's mother whom I called Grandma Vi. She was dealing with Alzheimer's, and Arriana said she could be a hand full. I do not remember the story she told me about her, but it was to demonstrate how much work was required to care for her. She mentioned my uncle, her dad, and how her mom had spoiled him. She continued, "Mama is trying to help me and Mitch; she has so much on her. I have to get better, Shayron." I was lost for words. I could only say, "You will. You will."

She talked about how the infection had taken all of her energy. But she was clear; she did not want to go back to the hospital. She said the kids would not be able to handle if she had to go back. I did my best to encourage and make her laugh. I felt something different after this conversation. The word I can use to best describe how she felt is "disgusted."

I was headed to Doak Campbell Stadium with Dennis for the FSU vs. Virginia Tech game. We had just pulled into a parking space when I got a call from my dad. Arriana was back in the hospital; they were placing her in ICU on a vent to give her large doses of antibiotics.

I had to call Auntie. She was tearful and explained that the infection was bad. It had not gotten better, and Arriana needed large doses of antibiotics. She was having problems breathing. She told me through tears that she had been having trouble walking. Arriana did not want to go back, but they convinced her she had to go to the hospital. The cancer was in her spine and spinal cord. My RN brain kicked in. Okay, first she would get the antibiotics and then they would do more chemo to address the metastasis. She needed the ventilation and rest, so she wouldn't tax her body and waste energy struggling to breathe. She would be fine after that.

We made it home from Florida. In the back of my mind, I celebrated because she made it through the weekend. Yeah, that was good news. My dad, my aunt Trish, my sister and I kept in touch all weekend. We encouraged each other; we prayed, and we agreed she would be okay.

I returned to work. I saw a few text messages between my sister and my niece. Had I heard about Arriana? Heard what? It was the afternoon, and I was drowned in work as usual; I had not heard anything. I spoke with my sister shortly after then my dad later. Arriana Latrecia Mills Daniels had transitioned to be with her God.

The memorial musical tribute was such a tribute to her. She loved to sing praises unto God. She loved to uplift and encourage. I was nervous that my sister was not there. She was the speaker in the family; she was the oldest grandchild. I was not comfortable speaking in front of people. I did not want to cry.

My heart was broken. It didn't seem right; she couldn't really be gone. I shared how the nine cousins from four brothers (her father included) were close. We spent precious time together. It built bonds and memories that I will always cherish.

I wanted Christopher and Sydney to know that their mom was not only a great mom and wife, but she was a great person. She had always been fun as a kid – kind, caring, and concerned about others. I wanted her brother, Ervin, my younger cousin to know we would be there for him.

I know her presence would always be in our family, I'm grateful for the witness she showed me. All her life, whatever she did for God she gave her all. I won't complain. I won't say no to His will for my life. I'm grateful for the strong soldier that she was. I am thankful she showed me how to deal with "distractions." Arriana, I know where you are.

Have you accepted Jesus Christ as Lord and Savior? Have you surrendered your life to Him? Only time will tell. I hope to see you in heaven.

CHAPTER 7

REFLECTION – STEPHANIE D. MILLS

I knew my cousin Ariana Daniel for over 45 years, longer than all of her other first cousins, longer than her baby brother Ervin, longer than her husband and children. Even though they lived with her every day or more often than I did, she was like a sister to me. Our fathers are brothers and we were raised seeing each other frequently on the weekends and summers with our grandparents.

I could talk about our experiences with her being the only child for many years before her brother came and how she used that to her advantage. I could tell the stories of how she always sang, "Lean on Me" during our talent shows and said when she grew up, she was going to have a station wagon with 10 children. But I won't tell those stories. Instead, I want to share what I experienced from afar as I prayed and believed God for the restoration of her health, as well as her deliverance during her journey, her battle against the attack of cancer and the treatments.

It was a few weeks or so after she celebrated her 49th birthday. I had spoken to her on that birthday, and she said she was going out to dinner with Mitch and the kids.

I got a call from my sister telling me we needed to pray. She said Arriana had called to tell her about what the doctor said regarding her lab work and the need to go to a hospital right away. She was not to drive because it would have been too dangerous. I thought about all that she had been doing in ministry to build up the Kingdom of God and her faithful service at church. This was an attack on her physical body. Warfare calls for warfare in prayer.

Not knowing the extent of the attack at the time, I began to pray for her. At that time, I was still recovering from my own health challenges, so I could relate to the uncertainty about one's own health. I had come face-to-face with my own mortality on a few occasions after fainting and losing consciousness, so I was hoping and praying for the best for Ariana. I asked my sister to keep me posted. I did not want to be nosy, but to offer specific prayers for what I saw in the spirit as an attack on a daughter of God.

I also knew what it felt like to have health challenges and not want to have it broadcasted or discussed, especially when all the details are not clear to you. Nevertheless, you appreciate the concerns of loved ones and true friends. It is not a pleasant thing to have to explain diagnoses that you barely understand yourself.

So, rather than going through the dilemma of deciding to visit or not to visit, to call or not to call, I chose to go to God.

I chose to have a talk with Jesus in my prayer closet. Whatever I was going to talk to God about pertaining to my cousin Arriana's health was not new information to Him because He knows the end from the beginning.

I made up my mind that God is all powerful and all knowing, so I would go through this journey with my cousin Arianna from afar with prayer, supplication, fasting, and faith.

Of course, during Arriana's journey – from her initial diagnosis, to needing a bone marrow donor, to chemo and radiation, to having a bone marrow transplant, to recovery and healing, I would have my moments of anger. I would ask God how and why He would allow one of His own with so much more life ahead of her, with young children and a loving marriage to be affected like this and so suddenly. Why would He let that happen when she was so dedicated to His ministry?

After each of my sister's phone calls and visits, she would provide me with updates on Arriana, and I would pray the specific prayers. I called on some major prayer warriors, several of whom were healed and restored from the point of death, to join me in prayer on Arriana's behalf. I also prayed that God would strengthen Mitch during this journey and wrap His arms around their beautiful children. I am forever grateful to several of my sisters in Christ because the prayers of the righteous availeth much.

CHAPTER 8

REFLECTION ~ CARLA PATRICK

Friend ~ A friend is an acquaintance. A person whom one knows and with whom one has a bond of mutual affection, typically inclusive of family relations.

Sister ~ A girl or woman in relation to other daughters and sons of her parents.

Divine Connection ~ A link, a joining, a relationship, a bond brought together and formed by God.

◆ October 27, 2017 ◆

It's Friday and like every morning, I begin the day with prayer and praise. I thank God for another day, His grace, His mercy, His faithfulness, His kindness, His protection and provision and for not giving me what I really deserve. Then I call the names of people needing special prayer. That's when it hit me that this is not like every other morning. Today is different, much different. Instead of getting dressed and heading to work, I'm attending your life celebration.

How did we get here? We prayed; we fasted, and our faith was strong. And you, so strong, so courageous, so full of faith, never doubting but always trusting the Lord. Even in your weakest time, you were everything God created you to be.

I was asked to make remarks, but I have so many emotions. What an honor, but how will I do it? I'm trying to be strong but inside, I'm a mess.

I know the woman you were, the life you lived, and my spirit reminds me that **God is,** and He will always be in control. You are His and He has chosen this time to elevate you. He has called you to the highest level of worship. There is absolutely no doubt that the angels are rejoicing as they welcome you into the Father's holy kingdom. And even though you are not here, your spiritual legacy continues because more than ever, your passing has caused my hope, faith, and belief in God to be strengthened. So, in my sadness, I praise God for you, your life, and our time. Hallelujah!

~ Breathe ~

Hmm, you're calling me earlier than usual. You're trying to sound chipper, but I can tell something is wrong. "I'm in the hospital; it's cancer. I have Leukemia." What? I don't think I heard you right and then you repeated it. Oh my God! I can't feel a thing; I'm numb. In my mind, I hear the words cancer, Leukemia. I'm tearing up. I can't breathe. I want to fall apart, but I must be strong for you. Re, she's my sister, and she needs me, my strength, and my prayers. Finally, I exhale, and you are telling me about the plan for your care. Little did you know that while you were talking, I was getting dressed. Laughing, you said: "What's that dinging in the background little girl?" And I said… "I'm on my way."

⊷ Reminiscing ⊷

It was my day to be your caregiver. I had arrived early because you had a doctor's appointment. Well, your hair and my reaction set the tone for the day. You had the biggest, cutest, curly fro I'd ever seen. You took one look at my facial expression and busted out laughing saying, "I know my sister has plenty to say about my hair." Well, after a few baby afro jokes, we left for your appointment. It was a good day; you even stayed awake the entire drive. On the way, we started to reminisce about our days in the choir and wouldn't you know it? One of the songs we used to sing came on and that's all we needed. I started singing, and you were directing, which was especially funny because I was driving, and you are sitting next to me, but we were working it. All we needed were our choir robes, and it would have really been on. *Y'all better sing! Sing choir!*

By the time we got to the doctor's office, you had a new burst of energy. All the breakfast eating, juice drinking, loud talking and constant laughing coming from your room had the nurses asking if they could come and join in on the fun. They probably thought we were just getting started, and so did we. But not even an hour later, we were both down for the count; out like a light, snoozeville, knocked out. Oh yeah, we were asleep. Now I can surely understand why you went to sleep; you were the patient, but why was I asleep? I guess that's what sisters do.

Nothing follows a good nap like a good lunch, and Olive Garden was our spot. We must have ordered everything on the menu and then came our usual match, "Let me pay." Laughing during the check tug of war let me know you were definitely getting your strength back. We worked with that check so much it was all crinkled up when we gave it to the waitress. Your hair was all big and fluffy, and I was just fluffy, but the round was over. And while I may have won, you put up a "sho-nuff" good fight.

All the way home, we talked about what a good day we had. Each time was better than the one before. We also vowed that when you got well enough, we were going to resume our monthly lunches, no excuses.

You timed me just right. Walking in the door, I got a text from you. You said you had such a good time and couldn't wait for us to do it again. But what really stays with me is when you thanked me for always being there for you, taking care of you and for doing things that only a sister would do. "Awe, you are welcome Sis, but the pleasure is all mine cause that's what we do."

⚜ Wedding Gown ⚜

It seems like we've always been there for each other. I honestly cannot remember a time when we were not friends or even how our relationship grew. One night, we're leaving choir rehearsal and the next day, I'm your maid of honor.

Every Thursday after choir rehearsal, we'd call and talk about everything. But this particular night was different. You said, "I need to talk to you about something as soon as we get home." I had no idea what was about to come next. The call started off normal enough, and then we started talking about how in a few months you were going to be *married*.

We laughed and then you said something that changed our relationship forever. "You are my best friend, and I really want you to be my maid of honor." Well, I was speechless, and we both just laughed because nothing shuts me up. I will never forget how totally overwhelmed I was with feelings of honor and excitement.

"You want me to be your maid of honor? Oh my God! Yes!" Well after about five minutes of crying and carrying on, my wedding attitude set in. I couldn't wait – flowing dresses, beautiful flowers, lovely wedding party wearing big smiles. Here we go, places everyone. I'm the maid of honor. Watch out now!

It's a Boy

I can't believe it. I'm going to be an aunt. It just doesn't get any better than this. My favorite sister and brother-in-love are having a baby. What? You want me to be in the room when you deliver. Oh my God! I guess it can get better.

Christopher Alexander. He is so handsome, healthy, and strong. Thank heavens for little boys!

It's a Girl

"A little girl! I can't stand it. I'm beside myself. Really, there are two of me." You couldn't stop laughing at my antics.

Arriana said, "Yes, I'm having a girl. I knew you were going to have a fit."

"Have you picked a name? I like Carla…just kidding."

"Sydney Michelle."

"I love it, and I know she's going to be as beautiful and special as you are. Would love to chat, but I've got to go. I have a niece to get ready for – so much shopping, so little time."

Later, when we finally met, I looked at her and said, "Hello, baby girl! She's beautiful just like I knew she would be."

✼ Hot Water ✼

I've never had surgery before, and I'm nervous as can be. My surgery is tomorrow, and I know I'm in trouble because I still haven't told Re. But her plate is already overflowing: a hubby, two babies, church, work, this list goes on. I know if I tell her, she'll be here trying to take care of me too. No, I'll just wait until after the surgery and then tell her; she's got enough to do.

"What! Surgery! Oh, you are going to get it little girl. Let me tell you one thing. I am *your* sister, and I'm going to be there no matter what." Lord, I didn't know I could be in such hot water. It took days for her to stop fussing and pointing that finger. But our sisterhood was everything. I remember Arriana coming over, and I was in pain. She sat on the bed with me and started to pray. Then she sang me to sleep. And when I woke up, there she was smiling at me because that's what sisters do.

⚜ The Calling ⚜

"For I can do everything through Christ, who gives me strength" (Philippians 4:13). I was not surprised when you said God had called you to preach the gospel. You had always been a woman after God's heart. I still remember your first sermon, "The Holding Pattern" and your favorite scripture, *"But they that wait upon the Lord shall renew their strength, they shall mount up with wings as eagles; they shall run, and not be weary, and they shall walk and not faint"* (Isaiah 40:31). From there, your ministry grew. You were called to preach and teach at several churches on many occasions. Your gifts and faithfulness to God continued to make room for you. At your church, you were the overseer of many ministries and faithfully served the members and your mom (the bishop) as assistant pastor. I watched you serve God and His people for as long as the Lord allowed. What a blessing!

⚜ Take My Hand ⚜

The day of my mom's service, you said, "Sis, take my hand," and you walked with me.

The day of my papa's service, you said, "Sis, take my hand," and you walked with me.

Now, today is your service, and I realize that you are not here to take my hand and walk with me. I cry. Then the Lord of comfort speaks to me, *"The LORD himself goes before you and will be with you; he will never leave you nor forsake you. Do not be afraid; do not be discouraged"* (Deuteronomy 31:8). In other words, "I am your Father. I'll walk with you; take My hand." Then all of a sudden, it was as if I could see your smiling face.

Even though you are no longer here physically, I could feel your presence and hear you saying "Sis, take my hand."

✧ Remarks ✧

These are the remarks I will share at the service on behalf of your sisters, Paula, Ty, and me. The first part of my remarks is from a poem I read and shared with you years ago. When asked to make remarks, I just knew I had to include it because it seemed like the person who wrote it knew you, knew me, knew us.

Remarks are very special; they're personal because they come from the heart. Many times, it's hard to put into words what a person really means to you. This is definitely one of those times.

Here we go:

To my family Mitch, Christopher, Sydney, Mom, Dad, Ervin, the Mills, and Daniel family. I say my family because Arriana, I call her Re, was more than a friend; she was my sister. When I was asked to make remarks, I got so caught up just reminiscing about all the times I shared with Arriana until finally, I realized that the love, bond, and sisterhood we shared was just too big to put into words. But I'm hoping that these few words speak to some of the many things she was to me.

Poem by Allison Chambers Coxsey

"We were blessed to call you sister; we also called you friend.

You loved us unconditionally. You were there through thick and thin.
We shared our joys and sorrows, laughter, and tears.
You were our inspiration as we grew over the years"
And what a joy it was to see the woman of God you came to be. Serving and singing, praying and praising, worshiping, and preaching, all the world could see.
God's Spirit was upon you, and He was using you for His Glory.
Too soon was the day when the Father whispered your name.
It broke our hearts to see you go because our lives were forever changed.
Sweetest are the memories, we'll always have of you,
And even though our hearts are broken and our eyes are filled with tears,
We thank God for the wonderful times we were blessed to share with you, over the years.
Family, thank you for sharing Arriana with us!
We love you!

Divine Connection

Divine Connection ~ a link, a joining, a relationship, a bond brought together and formed by God.

Bishop Mills or as I affectionately call you, Mama Fran, thank you for the light and life you gave us in the person of Rev. Arriana Mills Daniel. An *exceptional wife, mother, daughter, and sister, an extraordinary friend and an exemplary woman of faith.*

Thank you, Mama Fran, for your love and support, and for unselfishly including me in all things "Re." I consider it not only a privilege but an honor to be a part of this great work. It would be impossible to pen the totality of our sisterhood, but I hope by reading this chapter, you and countless others will experience the joy, tears, excitement, love, and bond that we shared. For many, this will be just a chapter in a book, but for me, it's a story of two friends, no, two sisters with a divine connection.

"But they that wait upon the Lord shall renew their strength, they shall mount up with wings as eagles; they shall run, and not be weary, and they shall walk and not faint" (Isaiah 40:31).

PART 3

FEARLESS ON THE JOURNEY

(A DAUGHTER'S MESSAGE TO THE WORLD)

CHAPTER 9

ARE YOU ANCHORED IN THE LORD?
(BY REV. ARRIANA MILLS DANIEL)

And when it was day, they knew not the land: but they discovered a certain creek with a shore, into the which they were minded, if it were possible, to thrust in the ship. And when they had taken up the anchors, they committed themselves unto the sea, and loosed the rudder bands, and hoisted up the mainsail to the wind, and made toward shore. And falling into a place where two seas met, they ran the ship aground; and the forepart stuck fast, and remained unmoveable, but the hinder part was broken with the violence of the waves. And the soldiers' counsel was to kill the prisoners, lest any of them should swim out, and escape. But the centurion, willing to save Paul, kept them from their purpose; and commanded that they which could swim should cast themselves first into the sea, and get to land: And the rest, some on boards, and some on broken pieces of the ship. And so, it came to pass, that they escaped all safe to land (Acts 27:39-44).

Are you anchored in the Lord? What does it mean to be anchored in the Lord? Let's first understand what an anchor is and its functions.

The word "anchor" has several definitions. An anchor is a person or thing that can be relied on for support, stability or security. The anchor of a boat is a piece of equipment that keeps a boat or ship steady or in its place. It prevents it from drifting. It's a source of security and stability. An anchor in a relay race is the person on a team who competes last, the one who brings up the rear. His responsibility is to close out the race or to secure the race for the team. An anchorman or woman is the main broadcaster on a news or sports program who usually serves, secures or draws the viewing audience to a particular program. A drywall anchor is a piece of equipment for holding an object or securing objects to the wall.

What do all these definitions have in common? The key word is "secure." The anchor's purpose is to secure or stabilize something. In the same respect, Christ wants us securely anchored in Him. How do you ensure that you are anchored in the Lord? To understand this, let us look at the life of Paul.

Before his conversion, Paul, then known as Saul, was a zealous Pharisee who unrelentingly persecuted the followers of Jesus Christ. According to the accounts in the book of Acts, around the year 36 A.D., Paul was on his way from Jerusalem to Damascus to arrest the followers of Jesus. His intention was to return with them as prisoners for questioning and possible execution in Jerusalem.

But the mission was aborted when on the journey Saul saw a blinding light. He fell to the ground and communicated directly with a divine voice – the voice of Jesus Christ. After his encounter, Paul, blinded by the light, spent three days in Damascus during which time he was miraculously healed through Ananias (See Acts 9:17). After being baptized and filled with the Holy Spirit, Saul's name was changed to Paul.

During Paul's life, many plots were hatched against him, especially by the Jews. They were constantly stirring up the crowd and inciting them to violence wherever Paul preached. During Paul's missionary journeys, which covered a span of 30 years, he was beaten and thrown into prison many times just as he had once persecuted the Christians.

In fact, Paul met with persecution on every missionary journey he made. He was stoned in the city of Lystra for healing a crippled man just as he had ordered the deacon Stephen to be stoned (See Acts 14:8-19; 7:58). On one of his visits to the temple in Jerusalem, Paul was confronted by the religious authorities for "defiling the holy place" by bringing in Gentiles. This incited a violent mob that seized Paul and threatened to kill him. The commotion caught the attention of the Roman guards who immediately took custody of Paul (see Acts 21:28-31).

Paul remained in custody for nearly two years. During this time, he appealed to the governor not to be tried in Jerusalem, arguing that he would not get a fair hearing there because of the religious authorities. Because he was a Roman citizen, he appealed to be heard by Caesar (See Acts 22:28; 25:11). Paul's appeal to be heard in Rome was finally granted (See Acts 27:1).

This brings us to our main scripture. At this point, Paul is in the custody of a centurion who is preparing to escort him on the long voyage to Rome with several other prisoners.

The first eight verses of Chapter 27 take Paul from Caesarea to a harbor on the island of Crete named Fair Havens, not far from the city of Lasea. The ship was forced to shelter here because of hurricane force winds. Optimum sea travel could only be made during the summer months of May to September. It was highly dangerous to sail between September and March. Paul's journey was in early October.

Acts 27:9-13 describes a crucial decision that had to be made concerning the journey. It was too late in the sailing season to travel to Rome by sea. The question was where would the ship dock for the winter months? Paul strongly urged them to remain where they were at Fair Havens. Since this was not the ideal place to spend the winter, the sailing conditions had since improved, and the weather looked fine, the captain decided to press on anyhow, ignoring Paul's plea.

Ask yourselves this critical question. Why do we need to be anchored in Christ? Most people recognize the need to be anchored; therefore, they attempt to anchor themselves to something. The issue is they anchor themselves to the wrong things or the wrong people. You can find people anchoring themselves to drugs, alcohol, gangs, friends, relationships, television or shopping, just to name a few.

It's all right to have close relationships with family and friends but if you put your total trust and salvation in them, you will certainly go astray. Friends, family, drugs or alcohol cannot save or deliver you from your circumstances. Yes, they can comfort you but only for a while. In the end, you're in the same boat that you were in before you went to that thing in the first place. There are a number of guarantees you may count on when you are anchored in the Lord.

Guarantees the Presence of God

Let's look back at Paul on this ship. Not long after the ship left Fair Havens, tempestuous waters rose up again and battered the vessel. Now they were in imminent danger of shipwreck, and they were all filled with a sense of foreboding. But through it all because Paul was in God's presence, He could still hear God speaking through an angel.

> *And when neither sun nor stars in many days appeared, and no small tempest lay on us, all hope that we should be saved was then taken away. But after long abstinence, Paul stood forth in the midst of them and said, Sirs, ye should have hearkened unto me, and not have loosed from Crete, and to have gained this harm and loss. And now I exhort you to be of good cheer: for there should be no loss of any man's life among you, but of the ship. For there stood before me this night the angel of God, whose I am, and whom I serve, saying, Fear not Paul; thou must*

be brought before Caesar: and, lo, God hath given thee all them that sail with thee (Acts 27:20-24).

Because Paul had a divine appointment in Rome, his safety was assured, and so were all those on board. That is why he could look at the raging sea and still confidently say, *"Wherefore, sirs, be of good cheer: for I believe God that it shall be as it was told me"* (Acts 27:25).

God wants to speak to each of us in the situations we are in today. Are you in a position to hear Him? How differently would you respond to the circumstances if you were confident that the presence of God was with you?

Paul was told by the angel not to be afraid. He told the passengers not to lose hope but to keep up their spirits. Paul encouraged the passengers aboard that God would do exactly what He had promised. Remember the words of Deuteronomy 31:6: *"Be strong and of a good courage, fear not, nor be afraid of them: for the Lord thy God, he it is that doth go with thee; he will not fail thee, nor forsake thee."* Here's a perfect example of God stepping into the situation in the midst of danger and speaking words of encouragement and hope.

As a believer, what makes you feel that God will not deliver you from your storms? Is it because you haven't done what God has told you to do? Is it because you haven't walked according to the Word? Or perhaps you haven't spent enough time in His presence to hear from Him?

Remember, Paul didn't always walk with the Lord. He had actually been going in the opposite direction persecuting the people of the Way. But Paul's life was turned around, and he turned his zeal to the Lord. Once Paul was touched by God, he was changed. He spent his days preaching the Word of God and sharing the love of Jesus Christ to all who were around him. You cannot be touched by God and still be the same person. You will change. Once you commit your life to God, your name is forever changed from sinner to saved.

Will you still mess up? Yes, you will. Will you still sin? Yes, you will. *"For all have sinned, and come short of the glory of God"* (Romans 3:23). Will you still experience trouble along the way? Yes, that's unavoidable. In this life, you will have trials and tribulations. But, once you accept the Lord Jesus Christ, regardless of the troubles, regardless of the situations that come your way, you are guaranteed security in Him.

So, even in the midst of the turbulent events taking place on the journey, Paul could still hear God speaking to him. For God was always with him. Why do you need to be anchored in the Lord? you ask. Because being anchored guarantees the presence of God.

Guarantees the Peace of God

Again, Paul was experiencing the same storm as the prisoners, the crew, and the guards. All around everyone is panicking. But look at Paul – calm, cool, and collected. Unlike his shipmates, Paul has not lost hope because the angel of God had appeared to him and told him not to be afraid. But more trouble is brewing. Once the sailors discerned from their soundings that they were approaching land, they decided to take things into their own hands. They knew that they needed to be in deeper water for a ship that size. If the ship got into shallow water, it would run aground. It had to stay in the deeper waters, while the smaller boat or skiff could bring them to shore.

The sailors knew they could not handle the ship in such stormy weather. The skiff, however, would be easier for them to maneuver. So, they collectively made the decision to abandon the ship and escape for shore in it. But, if they did, what would have happened to the passengers on board? They would be stranded and helpless. There would be no one capable of steering the ship. Any attempt for someone else to try it other than the expert crew would be disastrous.

Paul became aware of these sailors' intentions to jump ship and intervened. He addressed the centurion and soldiers and issued a direct order, *"Except these abide in the ship, ye cannot be saved"* (Acts 27:31). He appealed to the soldiers' sense of responsibility toward the passengers. Turning to the soldiers, he was in effect saying, "The sailors need to remain on this ship, for it is necessary for all of us to make it to shore together and to survive." The soldiers acted on Paul's command.

When do you abandon hope? When do you throw in the towel? When do you give up and say, "All hope is lost"? When do you know there is nothing else you can do?

Such is the human condition in today's turbulent world. People are disoriented because they face emotional, relational, social, and physical storms. No one, no one, hear me, *no one* can save you but God.

Paul recognized that, in these troubled waters all around them, there was no way they could be saved without

God. It is the same today. You cannot save yourself. There's no deed or work you can do to obtain salvation. It doesn't matter what you do or say. Only God can save you. Only God can deliver you. Only God can set you free.

Guarantees the Power of God

God's power was revealed to everyone on the ship. It was only when all hope was lost that Paul addressed his shipmates. Much time had lapsed as the storm lashed around them. They had not eaten for days in their furious efforts to save the ship. They had wrapped cords around the ship. They had buckled down the hatches trying to get to safety. Day in and day out, they battled the angry waves.

Oftentimes, you feel your troubles are endless. It seems as though you will never see the break of dawn with constant darkness and storms all around you. As soon as you leave one storm, there's another one coming right ahead. It seems hopeless. And then the next new day dawns.

> *And while the day was coming on, Paul besought them all to take meat, saying, This day is the fourteenth day that ye have tarried and continued fasting, having taken nothing. Wherefore I pray you to take some meat: for this is for your health: for there shall not an hair fall from the head of any of you* (Acts 27:33-34).

The new day indeed brought hope. Paul assured them that not a hair on their heads would be lost. He now gave some practical advice. If their safety was assured, they needed to eat to fortify themselves. Then he took bread, gave thanks to God and began to eat. Paul's faith and courage were contagious, and all the passengers began to eat. They were strengthened in body and spirit. Now they were ready for the race. They were ready to tackle the storm. They were ready to lighten the load.

What they started doing was throwing stuff overboard. They had to get things out of the way because the ship was too heavy. It needed to be lighter so that it could get as close as possible to shore.

In the same way, God wants you to lighten your load. He wants you to get rid of your burdens. Because He is omniscient and omnipotent. He oftentimes says, "I need you to get rid of these things that are holding you down and causing you to sink by their weight."

He is saying to get rid of despair! Get rid of grief! Get rid of fear and anxiety! Get rid of depression! Get rid of drug and sex addiction! Get rid of alcoholism! Get rid of everything that's holding you down. Get rid of all of these things that are keeping you from making it to where God wants you to be. Get rid of all of the things that won't let you move in the right direction. God wants you to get to the place He's trying to get you to. But you've got to get rid of some stuff.

Sometimes, you've got to get rid of some friends and coworkers. Sometimes, you've got to stop shopping so much and read the Word so that you can get back into a consistent relationship with God.

The more things you throw away that are holding you down, taking over your life and causing you despair, the more you will lighten your load. You will be able to weather the storm. You'll be able to hang in. You'll make it to shore. Throw away the worry, grief, and despair. Throw them all away so that God can use you.

Guarantees the Provision of God

> *But the centurion, willing to save Paul, kept them from their purpose; and commanded that they which could swim should cast themselves first into the sea, and get to land: And the rest, some on boards, and some on broken pieces of the ship. And so it came to pass, that they escaped all safe to land* (Acts 27:43-44).

In Roman times, if a soldier was in charge of any prisoners and they escaped, he would lose his life. The soldiers reasoned that the prisoners might escape, and they didn't want to suffer that penalty. So, they quietly plotted together: "We're getting close to shore, and we'd better not let these prisoners get away. How can we hold them back? Let's go and kill them now before they try to escape." But the centurion stopped them. He knew that Paul was a Roman citizen and had special rights under the law. "No, no, no," he said. "Don't do him any harm. Let him go!"

You see, the centurion had listened to Paul's words and was convinced that everybody was going to make it safely to shore. In so many words, the centurion then instructed all on board as follows: "All that you need to do is this. When we run aground, when the ship touches bottom, when the ship starts breaking up, everybody in the boat that can swim, jump first. The rest of you, even if you can't swim, it's okay; you're going to be safe anyway. When the ship starts breaking up, hang on to some piece. Get anything you see. Grab on to it. Ride with it to shore. Don't worry. We are all going to make it."

And, just as Paul had promised, not a soul was lost. 276 were on board. 276 made it to shore. Some on broken pieces – but they made it. Some on planks – but they made it. God's provision came through just as Paul had promised.

You, too, will not be lost when you're anchored in the Lord. No matter the situation, no matter the difficulty, the provision of God will come through right on time. When you're anchored, Christ gives you clear direction. He prevents the wrong decisions from being made. He eliminates worry and anxiety. He produces peacefulness and confidence. He sharpens your discernment. He gives you energy. He prevents distractions. He protects you from discouragement. He opens doors of opportunity.

God gave them the word of hope through Paul. Once a sinner, now a changed man – that's the power of divine grace. The power of grace is so evident in the new Paul who had once made it his mission to murder Christians. It demonstrates God's power to use anyone and everything to achieve His purpose, and for you to obtain yours, too.

To obtain our purpose, let's start by being unequivocally anchored in the Lord. Are you anchored in the Lord?

CHAPTER 10

HOLDING PATTERN
(BY REV. ARRIANA MILLS DANIEL)

But they that wait upon the Lord shall renew their strength; they shall mount up with wings as eagles; they shall run and not be weary; and they shall walk, and not faint (Isaiah 40:31).

Has there ever been a time in your life when you waited on God for an answer, deliverance or a breakthrough, but it seemed as if He was not listening to you? Did you feel as if He had forgotten about you and your situation? Have you ever thought, "Why am I in this situation? Why won't God just fix this and allow me to move on?"

Do you think your prayers, fasting, and seeking God for answers are useless? Does it appear as if the days, weeks, months, and even years of doing these things are a waste of time? It may seem as though you are in the same place, in this boat, and you're just going around in circles waiting in a holding pattern.

What is a holding pattern? *Webster Dictionary* defines a holding pattern as a state of inaction with no progress and no change, failure to advance, useless or unproductive activity. A holding pattern in aviation is the flight path maintained by an aircraft that is waiting for permission to land or takeoff. In aviation, a holding pattern or flying in a halt is designed to delay an aircraft's progress, keeping it within the specified airspace. It is a maneuver that consists of making the aircraft turn around and around or hold up at an assigned altitude or area while awaiting further air traffic controller instructions.

Many of us might liken this definition to our lives. At times, it seems as if we're in a useless, unproductive position. We're going around in circles, making no progress. We have found ourselves in a state of inaction, just waiting. But is that really such a bad state? I beg to differ from the idea that a holding pattern is a useless or unproductive position. While we might think we are in a time where there is no change and nothing is happening in our lives, Romans 8:28 tells us, *"All things work together for our good."*

The problem with many Christians is that we don't understand the seemingly circular turn of events. We don't see its value in our lives. We have not grasped the truth that these holding patterns are opportunities for us to wait on God to release us to our higher calling and purpose in life.

Let's dig a little deeper so we can understand the importance of such patterns. Air traffic controllers operate the air traffic control systems to expedite and maintain a safe and orderly flow of air traffic. They are the pilots' eyes and ears in the sky. Traffic controllers use radars to help them monitor all air traffic. Using the radar, they direct and position aircraft that are flying to and from various locations; they can see everything that's happening in the airspace. They know when the landing aircraft needs to fly, if there's trouble in the air or on the ground and if the aircraft needs redirecting. They can even see if there's a storm ahead.

Pilots, on the other hand, only fly or guide the aircraft. They are only authorized to move the aircraft with the permission of the air traffic controller. Have you ever wondered why the windows of the aircraft are so small? Pilots don't need to see where they are going except during takeoff and landing. They can only see what's directly in front of them and depend on the air traffic controller for instructions. In actuality, if it were not for the few minutes they take off and land, there would be no need for them to have windows in the aircraft at all. There's no need for sight during flight. In a sense, pilots fly by faith, not by sight. This is similar to how Christians operate. They walk by faith, not by sight.

At times, pilots and Christians are in the same position; they can see nothing. Sometimes, as Christians, we have no idea what's happening or what's next. We simply walk by faith.

Pilots flying aircraft in a storm oftentimes can't see. The clouds hinder their vision. They must fully depend on the air traffic controller to guide them through the storm to safety. They must also trust the air traffic controller to tell them how high or low to fly and whether to fly to the left or the right. Pilots do not make a move without the air traffic controller's permission. Why? They trust the relationship and the direction of the air traffic controller completely. Why am I consistently referencing the relationship between the pilot and the air traffic controller? There is a direct correlation between air traffic controllers and pilots and God with Christians.

God is omnipotent and omniscient. He sees and knows all. He knows our future. He understands that we have limited sight. We have no knowledge of what's ahead. He knows that inevitably; storms will come in our lives. Therefore, He wants us to seek Him for direction and guidance. He wants us to fully trust Him. He doesn't want us to lean on our limited vision and try to figure out what's happening. Rather, He desires that we have faith in Him and be confident that He will take care of us.

Many steps and procedures have to be followed prior to an aircraft taking off. First, the relationship is built between the pilot and the air traffic controller. The air traffic controller discusses the flight plan. He talks about the weather, and he usually goes through issues that may arise during the flight. Generally, he ensures that the pilot has knowledge of the plan.

It would be unusual, and I dare say frightening, if a pilot just jumped into an aircraft and took off. Of course, he would be breaking civil aviation rules and regulations but more importantly, he would endanger the lives of many people including his. A good pilot never does that! He checks the aircraft carefully and ensures that all instruments are functioning properly. Pilots get to know the aircraft they are preparing to fly.

Like pilots and air traffic controllers, if we want to be successful, it is essential to have a relationship with God. We must get to know Him personally. Instead of jumping into situations, going in our own directions or trying to buy this or that, we should seek the plan God has for us and get to know it. Of course, the pertinent question is how do we get to know God's plan? The answer is simple: we spend time with God. Read, study, and pray. Choosing to follow these instructions will help you during your holding pattern.

God Wants Us Engaged

God wants us to be fully engaged and in dialogue with Him on a regular basis. Galatians 6:6 says, *"Anyone who is taught or receives instructions in the word must share or communicate all things with his instructor, God."*

Pilots spend a number of years training and learning how to fly. They study manuals, understand wind velocity, and go through various levels of training and education. They learn how to fly different types of aircraft, the speed required to take off and land, how to read the instruments located in the aircraft, how to monitor speed, as well as weights and altitudes. To fly an aircraft, pilots must first understand the job and what it takes to keep the aircraft in the air.

After satisfying the civil aviation authorities that they have had adequate training and understand how to fly, they receive licenses. The license itself is an indication the person knows how to fly and understands the rules of flying. You cannot fly an aircraft if you don't read and understand the manual. Like pilots, Christians are expected to spend time studying, learning, developing, and understanding the Word of God.

What is God's manual? The Bible. However, most Christians don't want to spend time studying the Word. Instead, we fool ourselves that we can just get on the plane and go. In other words, we get up in the morning and go on our way without a license. We want to do our own thing and sing like the old Frank Sinatra melody "I Did It My Way." We feel because we've been to church, heard the priest deliver a message, the choir singing a good song and the deacon praying a long prayer, "Oh, I'm ready now. I'm equipped to do what I got to do." That is so far from the truth.

The message, song, and prayer are good. In fact, they can give us a little pep in our steps and some motivation here and there, but that will barely sustain us. They are like the peanuts and chips we get when we go on an airplane. It's not enough food to fill us up. Truth is it's just enough to get you to the next stop.

Christians must understand we have a responsibility to read, study, pray, and spend time alone with God to understand the manual He has given us. Understanding the manual initiates growth and takes us to new levels. It allows us to defeat the odds and live in peace and purpose. The Bible, our manual, is invaluable. What it simply means is what I am. God gave us this guidebook as our compass to maneuver in this life. It teaches us how to live, where, when and how to go.

God Wants Us Equipped for the Task

"The great shepherd of the sheep equips you with everything good for doing his will" (Hebrews 13:21). Pilots must be attentive to the instructions given by the air traffic controller. Doing

otherwise could lead to a disaster, not only for the pilot but everybody in his care. Everyone is affected by the pilot's decisions: those on the ground, in the plane, families, and friends. If the air traffic controller says, "Hold up. You can't land right now," but the pilot says, "I'll do what I want to do" and lands the plane anyway, what do you think will happen? Most likely, the plane will crash. Who is affected? Everybody.

Just as it is essential for the pilot to be attentive and follow the air traffic controller's instructions, it is equally important for the believer to follow God. God gives us clear directions to keep us away from danger. The air traffic controller sees what's on the radar; likewise, Christ can see what's on our radar. Hence, when we choose to go in a different direction, do things our way and not see the will of God, it usually leads to disaster. Our decisions, like the pilot's, affect those around us.

If you have a family depending on you and you decide to quit your job, what's going to happen? Everybody's going to suffer. You won't be equipped to support your family financially. Similarly, if you fail to be equipped by following God's instructions, you put yourself, your family and others at risk.

God Wants Us to Follow

God expects us to follow Him. *"Blessed are they who keep His statutes and seek Him with all His heart"* (Psalms 119:2). The air traffic controller has a clear picture of what's going to happen with the aircraft. Hence, he is the best person to instruct the pilot how to land the plane safely. When the gate is down, the controller knows it's not ready for the aircraft. Therefore, to avoid an accident on the ground, trouble or congestion, he delays the aircraft from landing and holds it in place. That is what we call the holding pattern.

The passengers can see the airport ahead. They are anxious to land. Perhaps, some may have connecting flights; others may be eager to see their families or to get to a job. However, if the air traffic controller says do not land, according to the rules, the pilot can't land the plane. In the interest of safety, he has to wait.

God is like the air traffic controller directing our lives. Sometimes, He places a holding pattern on each of us to save us from danger. He says, "You must wait." Like the pilot, we must have faith in God's instructions knowing there is a reason for our holding pattern.

One time, the bishop and I were returning home from Ohio. We boarded the plane. It appeared to be ready for takeoff. All our bags and everything were on the plane. Unexpectedly, the pilot said on the intercom, "I'm sorry folks. We're going to have a delay for a moment. We can't take off right now. We're going to have to wait." We waited in our holding pattern on the tarmac for an hour. Eventually, the aircraft was given permission to take off. The plane was then redirected to Kentucky.

Little did we know that there were storms raging all up and down the East Coast at that time. To protect us from the tornadoes that were touching down all around us, the air traffic controller redirected us to Kentucky. Our flight that normally would have only taken two hours took us two days because when we got to Kentucky, we had to stay in Kentucky. They would not allow us to board another plane heading to Atlanta because of the storms that were heading there. We waited until the next morning to get on our flight headed back to Atlanta. We were protected from unseen dangers. We had no clue what was happening around us until we landed in Kentucky.

God sees what's ahead. He knows if the job is ready for you. That's your holding pattern. He knows if someone else is in the position or in your house that He's preparing for you. That's your holding pattern. He knows that you took that job today and the company is going to fall tomorrow. That's your holding pattern. He knows all about your situations.

Most of the time, we get held up because of the stuff that we do. But there are times in our lives when God places us in a holding pattern. These are the times when He is trying to get our attention to develop a relationship with us. However, we are too impatient, and we barge ahead not seeking God's direction, not waiting for Him to clear our paths to remove any dangers from the landing strip in the gate.

Every time we move ahead of God, there is a disaster. All of us can think of times when we made bad choices; we made bad decisions. Those decisions affected our spouses, children, parents, and everyone around us.

We must always seek direction from God before making a move. God wants us to understand that He has our best interest at heart. You may not realize it, but He could be trying to protect you from dangers you don't even see ahead of you. We could not see the storms and tornadoes when we were delayed in Ohio, but the air traffic controller could. Likewise, the omnipotent, omnipresent, and omniscient God sees everything ahead of you. In His love and wisdom, He will do everything He can to protect you. But for you to be safe, He expects you to follow Him.

God Knows Your Ending

"I know the plans I have for you, says the Lord that are plans for good and not for disaster, to give you a future and a home" (Jeremiah 29:11). The holding pattern or our having to wait is not easy. Your patience and faith are tested time and time again. It is in the waiting though that our faith grows. During the holding pattern, all we should do is wait. God is simply trying to get our undivided attention, so He can speak to us. During the holding patterns, God can show us things about ourselves that we never would have understood or seen before. The purpose of the holding pattern is to prepare us for what's ahead, strengthen us for the journey, humble us, protect us, develop our faith, allow God time to speak to us, get our attention, purify us from sin, call us to surrender to Him, conform us to His image, equip us to serve Him, and prepare us for the blessing.

When we wait on the Lord and endure our holding pattern, our strength will be renewed. *"They that wait upon the Lord shall renew their strength"* (Isaiah 40:31). If you're tired of waiting on the Lord, don't worry, He will renew your strength. Have you ever seen an eagle's wings? They stretch seven feet wide and weigh 12 pounds. Have you ever seen how they soar in the air; how wide they are and how high they can fly?

If you just wait on the Lord, you will mount up on wings like eagles from your troubles. You're going to fly above your enemies and all your situations. Stay in your holding pattern until God tells you to move.

"You shall walk and not faint" (See Isaiah 40:31). If you wait on the Lord, victory, peace, love, and joy will be yours.

God has a purpose, plan, and process for everything you're going through. He is always there. God never leaves your side, not for a moment, hour or day. If you find yourself in a holding pattern, pray and wait for God. Ask Him for the grace to live your life productively. Despite your situation, you will arrive safely. Your present position is not your final destination. Before you know it, it will be time for you to land.

Our holding patterns make us strong and patient. We are guided by the all-wise God. We cannot crash when we follow His instructions and draw closer to Christ. Therefore, hold on to God's unchanging hand and know that in the holding pattern, God catches you. Do not get weary. God will mount you up, and you will fly above every issue you encounter. Wait, I say, on the Lord.

We are grateful that we have air traffic controller Jesus, on our side. Without Him, we would not know what to do. Have you been held up? Have you been stopped? Have you been in a circular motion and can't figure out why you are still there? Why can't you get off the treadmill? God wants you to know it's your time. Trust in Him. Give Him your heart today.

God says, "I'm here. I know all about it. I can see the radar, and I know what you're going through. I'm here to cover you, and I am ready to help you understand every holding pattern in your life. I purposefully place you in a *holding pattern* until I see that it is safe for you to land!

PART 4

THE AUTHORS ON THE JOURNEY

ABOUT THE AUTHORS

Reverend Arriana Mills Daniel

Reverend Arriana Mills Daniel was born and raised in Decatur, Georgia to Mr. Ervin E. and Bishop Frances V. Mills. She is the oldest of two children. She has been married to Mr. Mitch Daniel for 15 years and they are the proud parents of Christopher Alexander and Sydney Michelle.

Arriana was a 1985 honor graduate of Avondale High School in Decatur, Georgia. She received her bachelor's degree in Business Administration from the University of Georgia and her master's degree in Human Resources Management from Keller University. Arriana entered the corporate business world as a Financial Aid Officer with DeVry Institute in Atlanta. After serving at DeVry for several years, she left to accept a position with ITC as Assistant Director of Admissions. Later she would join the leadership team at Atlanta Technical College where she served as Dean over several departments and managed 90 employees until she stepped away from her position to start and run her own businesses. She was the Founder and CEO of 2 businesses – "Fashions by Nichelle" and "Emerging Visions Consulting, Inc."

Arriana accepted the Lord at an early age at The Greater Piney Grove Baptist Church, where she served faithfully for over 32 years. She joined the Tabernacle of Faith Christian Church in September 2005 and while at Tabernacle, was committed to serving the Lord and His people in any way He saw fit. In August 2007, she was ordained a Deacon. In 2009, she accepted her call to ministry and in October 2010 was licensed to preach the Gospel. In November 2014, she was ordained as a Minister of the Gospel and was promoted to the position of Assistant Pastor and a member of the Executive Board. She also served as Minister of Music, was the overseer of the Youth and Children activities. She also served as a member of the Finance Team and was the church Membership Secretary.

Arriana always said "I am truly humbled that the Lord has now called me to yet another level of service and elevation. Great is the Lord and greatly to be praised for the things He has done."

Her motto was *"But they that wait upon the Lord shall renew their strength, they shall mount up with wings as eagles; they shall run, and not be weary, and they shall walk and not faint"* (Isaiah 40: 31).

Bishop Frances V. Mills

Bishop Frances Virgil Mills is a native of Waycross, Georgia. She accepted the Lord as her personal Savior at an early age at Big Bethel Freewill Baptist Church in Waycross. She recommitted her life to the Lord in 1973 at The Greater Piney Grove Baptist Church in Atlanta, Georgia. She acknowledged her call to ministry in April 1997; was licensed to preach the gospel in January 1998 and was ordained in November 1999 under the pastorate of Rev. Dr. William E. Flippin, Sr. at The Greater Piney Grove Baptist Church. In September 2005, Bishop Mills became the founder and Pastor of Tabernacle of Faith Christian Church in Decatur, Georgia.

In 2010, Bishop Mills was recognized and honored as "Woman of the Year" for her service to the community by the Ross Report News. In 2013, she was consecrated to the office of "Bishop" under the leadership of Archbishop Ruth W. Smith. In 2018, she was honored as a Woman in Ministry Trailblazer.

Bishop Mills has been an active leader in the Metro Atlanta community where she served in the Mount Calvary Missionary & Education Baptist Association for more than 20 years. She was appointed to the position of 1st Vice Moderator – making her the first female to hold a leadership position in this 70-plus-year-old organization.

Bishop Mills has been married to Bro. Ervin E. Mills, her high school sweetheart and her greatest supporter in ministry, for 52 years. She and Bro. Mills are the proud parents of two children – Ervin Allen Curtis Mills and the late Rev. Arriana Mills Daniel. They are the proud grandparents of six – Keyona, Ervin Allen Curtis II, Jazmin, Christopher, Sydney and Keyshon and proud great grandparents of Sophia Arriane Mills.

Bishop Frances V. Mills is a woman of God – called to serve, constrained by love, convicted by the Word, consecrated by the blood, confirmed by the gospel, controlled by the Holy Ghost and committed to equipping the saints through teaching and preaching the gospel of Jesus Christ!

Her motto is: *"I can do all things through Christ who strengtheneth me"* (Philippians 4:13).

CONTACT INFORMATION
404-310-6851
revfvmills@aol.com
www.tabernacleoffaithcc.org

www.ingramcontent.com/pod-product-compliance
Lightning Source LLC
Chambersburg PA
CBHW030330080526
44584CB00012B/789